What Are They Saying About Matthew's Sermon on the Mount?

Warren Carter

PAULIST PRESS
New York / Mahwah, N.J.

ACKNOWLEDGMENTS
The Publisher gratefully acknowledges use of the following materials: quotations taken from *The Sermon on the Mount* by Robert Guelich, copyright © 1982 by Word Incorporated, Dallas, Texas. Used with permission; and a reproduction of a chart entitled "The Unity of the Sermon" from M.D. Goulder, *Midrash and Lection in Matthew,* copyright © 1974 by SPCK Publishing, London, England.

Library of Congress Cataloging-in-Publication Data

Carter, Warren, 1955–
    What are they saying about Matthew's Sermon on the mount? / Warren Carter.
        p. cm.
    Includes bibliographical references.
    ISBN 0-8091-3473-X
    1. Sermon on the mount—Criticism, interpretation, etc.—History. 2. Bible. N.T. Matthew V-VII—Criticism, Interpretation. etc.--History. 3. Sermon on the mount—Criticism, Redaction. 4. Bible. N.T. Matthew V-VII—Criticism, Redaction. I. Title.
    BT380.2.C35 1994
    226.9'06'09045—dc20   94-2720
                                                         CIP

Published by Paulist Press
997 Macarthur Boulevard
Mahwah, New Jersey 07430

Printed and bound in the
United States of America

Contents

For Janet
with thanks

Abbreviations

ATLA	American Theological Library Association
BEvTh	Beiträge zur evangelischen Theologie
BJRL	*Bulletin of the John Rylands Library*
CBQ	*Catholic Biblical Quarterly*
Eph Th L	*Ephemerides Theologicae Lovanienses*
ExposT	*Expository Times*
FBBS	Facet Books, Biblical Series
IBS	*Irish Biblical Studies*
ICC	International Critical Commentary
JAAR	*Journal of the American Academy of Religion*
JBL	*Journal of Biblical Literature*
JSNTSS	Journal for the Study of the New Testament Supplement Series
NCB	New Century Bible
NovT	*Novum Testamentum*
NTD	Das Neue Testament Deutsch
NTS	*New Testament Studies*
OBO	Orbis biblicus et orientalis
SBS	Stuttgarter Bibelstudien
SNTSMS	Society for New Testament Studies Monograph Series

THKNT	Theologischer Handkommentar zum Neuen Testament
TS	*Theological Studies*
TZ	*Theologische Zeitschrift*
WMANT	Wissenschaftliche Monographien zum Alten und Neuen Testament
WUNT	Wissenschaftliche Untersuchungen zum Neuen Testament

Introduction

The Sermon on the Mount, found in chapters 5–7 of Matthew's gospel, is one of the best-known sections of the New Testament. This volume in the "What Are They Saying About . . . ?" series surveys and evaluates what some contemporary scholars are saying about the Sermon on the Mount. Several factors have guided the selection of material to be discussed in this book.

First, consistent with the aims of this series, I will focus on material published since 1960. Such a survey is overdue for several reasons. The last major reviews of scholarship on the Sermon on the Mount date from the 1960's.[1] Recent discussions of Matthean studies have included aspects of the Sermon on the Mount but without being comprehensive.[2] A glance at the periodical indices and at recently published books (including commentaries on Matthew's gospel) indicates that scholars continue to debate aspects of the Sermon and offer fresh interpretations. It is timely to survey this current debate.

A second factor, the pervasive use of *redaction criticism* during this time, makes a review of scholarship since the 1960's appropriate.[3] Redaction criticism is concerned with the way in which each gospel writer shapes or redacts tradi-

1

tions about Jesus. Redaction critics view the gospel writers as creative pastoral theologians who interpret traditions about Jesus to address the needs of their particular communities of faith. Redaction critics moved the focus of form criticism on the pre-gospel forms and transmission of traditions about Jesus (in the time between 30–70 CE) to the interpretive contribution of the gospel writers in the 70's and 80's.[4]

In 1960 a book entitled *Tradition and Interpretation in Matthew* was published which contained studies on Matthew's gospel by Günther Bornkamm, Gerhard Barth and Heinz Joachim Held.[5] This volume was a trail-blazing work because it used redaction criticism to discuss Matthew's shaping of traditions. This method has dominated the discussions of the Sermon since the early 1960's.[6]

The dominant position of redaction criticism in gospel studies is, though, now being challenged by new methods. Some recent contributions are employing literary, narrative, or reader-response criticisms. These methods focus on the finished form of the gospel texts, rather than on the author's particular contributions in reshaping the sources.[7] Attention moves from author to reader, from sources to finished text, from individual units to the unity of the gospel narrative. In a time of emerging new methods, it is helpful to evaluate the scholarship of the last thirty years.[8]

A third factor points to the appropriateness of a survey of scholarship on the Sermon on the Mount since 1960. In 1963, W. D. Davies published *The Setting of the Sermon on the Mount*,[9] which has significantly influenced subsequent scholarship. Davies builds explicitly on the emerging redaction-critical understanding of the gospel authors as creative shapers of traditions about Jesus to identify aspects of Matthew's situation which influenced the composition of the Sermon.[10] The scope of Davies' book is wide-ranging. Its insistence on the socio-historical setting of the Sermon counters views of the Sermon as a set of timeless principles. Davies draws attention to diversity within the Christian movement and to interaction with its Jewish context, especially messianic expectation and events in contemporary Judaism. He emphasizes the Sermon's connection to the rest of Matthew's gospel highlighting the relationship of God's gift and demand, of law and grace.

Reviewers recognized that Davies' book was a major contribution because of its expansive scope, learning and conclusions. During the last thirty years, many have disagreed with various parts of it, but scholars have continued to be in frequent dialogue with it and the issues it addressed. Its appearance in the early 1960's further marks that time as initiating a distinct period of scholarship on the Sermon.

Two other factors have influenced my choice of material for this book. I have identified important areas of discussion in the current debate as well as the significant voices in those discussions.[11] This book can, therefore, act as a map for the field, as a guide for the reader's further engagement with the ongoing dialogue about the Sermon.

It will be clear that I do not always agree with the authors I choose to discuss. Yet I and others have learned much from all these contributions and they are worthy of engagement. I have tried to be fair in summarizing and evaluating the contents. No doubt my own biases appear and others would disagree with what I have included or omitted and how I (and others) assess it.

Second, I have largely, though not exclusively, restricted my selection to English-language scholarship. I have done this because my hope is that readers will want to read the work discussed in the text or referred to in the notes. Yet important contributions and perspectives have originated from outside the English-speaking world. So I have included some German and French works to indicate the extensive nature of the discussion of the Sermon. A recognition of the

international nature of the dialogue about the Sermon reminds us that the Sermon itself originated from outside our
historical and cultural world.

With respect to the organization of this book, the
selection of chapters is governed by issues that have been
important over the last thirty years. We begin with the
sources of the Sermon, a significant question for redaction
critics. We move in chapter 2 to the structure of the Sermon. How have scholars understood the way in which Matthew organizes and shapes the material? This question
raises some further issues, especially the function or purpose of the Sermon in relation to the particular situation of
Matthew's readers. Chapter 3 looks at some ways of understanding this situation and how the Sermon might have addressed it. Chapters 4 and 5 focus on the content of the
Sermon. Scholars have interpreted key sections of the Sermon in different ways and I outline some of this diversity.
In these chapters I consider questions of the content and
function of the beatitudes, the relationship between Matthew's Jesus and the Mosaic traditions expressed in the antitheses, the content of the Lord's Prayer, and the ethical
implications of the Sermon.

The inclusion of the word "Matthew" in the book's title
may seem redundant to some since the Sermon on the
Mount appears only in this gospel (Luke has a Sermon on
the Plain, Lk 6:17, 20–49). However "Matthew" is included
to remind readers that the Sermon on the Mount belongs to
the larger unit of Matthew's gospel. I will give relatively little
attention to Luke's Sermon on the Plain and to the historical
Jesus (see Chapter 1).

In some ways, the task of writing this book has been a
daunting one. There is so much material to consider in limited
space; much of it shows a remarkable depth of insight, exegeti-
cal skill and theological perception impossible to reproduce in

this format. Yet I have thoroughly enjoyed reading new, and rereading familiar, discussions. I have been very aware of my debt to scholars and teachers like Terry Falla, Paul W. Meyer, J. Christiaan Beker and Steven Kraftchick who over a number of years have helped me understand a little of this and other New Testament texts. I am deeply appreciative for the editorial support offered by Lawrence Boadt of Paulist Press and for Dr. Stan Saunder's insightful responses to an earlier manuscript. I am also especially grateful to my student assistant Sandra MacFarlane for her research and editorial work. She will understand my very selfish wish that she not graduate for a long time!

In working on this material, time and again I have been aware that as scholars ask questions about the purpose and meaning of this very old and important text, it asks questions about our purpose and meaning. As we try to interpret this text, it continues to interpret us. I hope that this brief survey will contribute usefully to that ongoing task and interaction.

Notes

1. Harvey McArthur, *Understanding the Sermon on the Mount* (London: Epworth, 1961); Joachim Jeremias, *The Sermon on the Mount* (FBBS; Philadelphia: Fortress, 1963). It first appeared in German in 1959 and English in 1961. Warren Kissinger (*The Sermon on the Mount: A History of Interpretation and Bibliography* [ATLA Bibliography Series, No. 3; Metuchen, NJ: Scarecrow Press and The American Theological Library Association, 1975]) begins his survey with the *Didache*. His bibliography contains items which appeared in the 1970's though he does not discuss these in his history of interpretation which ends with McArthur and Davies. Clarence Bauman (*The Sermon on the Mount: The Modern Quest for its Meaning* [Macon: Mercer University, 1985]) surveys work from Tolstoy through to the 1960's. Other discussions are more

selective. Ursula Berner (*Die Bergpredigt: Rezeption und Auslegung im 20. Jahrhundert* [Göttingen: Vandenhoeck und Ruprecht, 1979]) focuses on twentieth century scholarship; Robert Guelich ("Interpreting the Sermon on the Mount," *Interpretation* 41 [1987] 117–130) surveys representative interpretations of the Sermon from throughout the history of the church. Ulrich Luz (*Matthew 1–7: A Commentary* [Minneapolis: Augsburg, 1989]) pays attention to the history of interpretation of particular sections. Charles E. Carlston ("Recent American Interpetation of the Sermon on the Mount," *Bangalore Theological Forum* XVII [1985] 9–22) discusses the work of W. D. Davies, Guelich and Hans Dieter Betz.

2. See Graham Stanton, *A Gospel for a New People: Studies in Matthew* (Edinburgh: T & T Clark, 1992); Robert France, "Matthew's Gospel in Recent Study," *Themelios* 14 (1989) 41–46; David Bauer, "The Interpretation of Matthew's Gospel in the Twentieth Century," in *Summary of Proceedings of the 1988 Forty-Second Annual Conference of the American Theological Library Association* (ed. Betty A. O'Brien, 1988) 119–145; Graham Stanton, "The Origin and Purpose of Matthew's Gospel: Matthean Scholarship from 1945 to 1980," *Aufstieg und Niedergang der römischen Welt* II.25.3 (ed. W. Haase; Berlin and New York: Walter de Guyter, 1985) 1890–1951; Donald Senior, *What Are They Saying About Matthew?* (New York/Ramsey: Paulist, 1983); Daniel Harrington, "Matthean Studies Since Joachim Rohde," *The Heythrop Journal* 16 (1975) 375–88.

3. Pioneering works include Willi Marxsen, *Der Evangelist Markus. Studien zur Redaktionsgeschichte des Evangeliums* (Göttingen: Vandenhoeck und Ruprecht, 1956, 1959); in English, Marxsen, *Mark the Evangelist* (New York and Nashville: Abingdon, 1969); Hans Conzelmann, *The Theology of St. Luke* (London: Faber and Faber, 1960). The German version, *Die Mitte der Zeit*, appeared in 1954. For discussion, see Norman Perrin, *What is Redaction Criticism?* (Philadelphia: Fortress, 1970); Joachim Rohde, *Rediscovering the Teaching of the Evangelists* (Philadelphia: Westminster, 1968).

4. Edgar V. McKnight, *What is Form Criticism?* (Philadelphia: Fortress, 1969).

5. Günther Bornkamm, Gerhard Barth and Heinz Joachim Held, *Tradition and Interpretation in Matthew* (London: SCM, 1963, 1971). The German version, *Überlieferung und Auslegung im Matthäusevangelium*, appeared in 1960. The volume includes Bornkamm's short study of Mt 8:23–27 which first appeared in 1948.

6. For a recent use of the method, Kari Syreeni, *The Making of the Sermon on the Mount* (Helsinki: Suomalainen Tiedeakatemia, 1987).

7. To name several significant contributions, David Rhoads and Donald Michie, *Mark as Story: An Introduction to the Narrative of a Gospel* (Philadelphia: Fortress, 1982); Jack Dean Kingsbury, *The Christology of Mark's Gospel* (Philadelphia: Fortress, 1983); R. A. Culpepper, *Anatomy of the Fourth Gospel: A Study in Literary Design* (Philadelphia: Fortress, 1983); Jack Dean Kingsbury, *Matthew as Story* (Philadelphia: Fortress, 1986); Robert Tannehill, *The Narrative Unity of Luke-Acts*, 2 vols. (Philadelphia and Minneapolis: Fortress, 1986, 1990). For explanation and assessment, Stephen Moore, *Literary Criticism and the Gospels: The Theoretical Challenge* (New Haven: Yale University, 1989); Mark Allan Powell, *What is Narrative Criticism?* (Minneapolis: Fortress, 1990). For a focus on Matthew, see the articles by Powell, Kingsbury, and David Bauer in *Interpretation* 46 (1992) 341–67; David Bauer, *The Structure of Matthew's Gospel: A Study in Literary Design* (JSNTSS 31; Sheffield: Almond, 1988); David B. Howell, *Matthew's Inclusive Story* (JSNTSS 42; Sheffield: JSOT, 1990); Herman Waetjen, *The Origin and Destiny of Humanness* (Corte Madera, CA: Omega, 1976) 15–25.

8. For discussion, Stanton, *Gospel*, 23–110. He urges the continuing use and central place of redaction criticism "complemented by other methods" (23, also 5–6).

9. W. D. Davies, *The Setting of the Sermon on the Mount* (Cambridge: Cambridge University, 1963).

10. Davies, *Setting*, 13, n.1.

11. Note the issues identified by Stanton (*Gospel*, 296) in his survey of scholarship on the Sermon: the relationship of Jesus to Moses, the relationship of grace and law, the addressees of the Sermon, the nature of the Sermon's language, the place of eschatology.

1
The Sources of the Sermon on the Mount

Matthew's gospel was probably written in the decade of the 80's in the first century.[1] In this chapter, our attention focuses on the time before the finished form of Matthew's Sermon on the Mount. Where did the content of the Sermon on the Mount originate? What were Matthew's sources? These questions have been important for redaction critics interested in identifying Matthew's distinctive theological perspectives from the way in which he shapes or redacts existing material.[2]

Four types of answers have been suggested: i) Matthew composed the Sermon as he wrote his gospel; ii) the Sermon already existed, either as a whole or in part, before the gospel was written; iii) it came word-for-word from Jesus of Nazareth crucified about the year 30; iv) some combination of the above possibilities. Most scholars advocate the fourth option, proposing that, as with the rest of the gospel, Matthew creatively shapes and interprets material passed on to him by early Christian communities.

Understanding how scholars identify the sources of the

Sermon on the Mount requires knowledge of the much larger discussion of the sources of the synoptic gospels (the gospels of Matthew, Mark and Luke). I will sketch this larger debate briefly and then look specifically at the sources of the Sermon.

The Synoptic Problem

Investigating the sources of the synoptic gospels and of the Sermon forms part of the inquiry into the perplexing similarities and differences among the synoptic gospels. Explaining these similarities and differences is called the synoptic problem. Scholars have tried to identify the order in which the three gospels were written and the relationships which may exist among them.

Most accept the Two-Source Hypothesis as the explanation for the similarities and differences among the three gospels. This theory developed through the nineteenth and twentieth centuries. It asserts that because of factors of length, order of material and similar content, Mark was the first gospel to be written and was a source used by Matthew and Luke.

Scholars have also noticed that Matthew and Luke share about two hundred verses which are mostly sayings of Jesus not in Mark. From the similarities of wording, order and type of material in these verses, many have concluded that Matthew and Luke drew this material from a common source which Luke usually represents more accurately. This second source is called "Q" (short for the German word "Quelle" which means "source").

Mark and "Q" are, then, the two sources referred to by the term Two-Source Hypothesis.[3] Two further sources, "M" and "L," have been suggested to account for material special to Matthew and to Luke which does not derive from Mark or "Q."[4]

The Two-Source Hypothesis, though, is not unanimously supported. Since the 1950's, a group of scholars, led particularly by William Farmer, has forced a rethinking of what some had declared to be "an assured result."[5] Farmer's 1964 book, *The Synoptic Problem*, built on the 1950s' work of B. C. Butler and raised questions about the adequacy of a number of aspects of the accepted solution.[6] For instance, the observation that most of Mark appears in Matthew and Luke does not necessarily point to Marcan priority but only to an intermediary role for Mark. Some have argued that the places in which Matthew and Luke share common material do not indicate the existence of "Q" but Luke's use of Matthew. As a result, there has been new interest in an alternative explanation, that Matthew was the first gospel, followed by Luke who knew Matthew, and then Mark who used both. This suggestion revives a theory advocated by Johann Griesbach in the late eighteenth century.

Farmer's work has created much debate with a series of conferences, working groups and publications. The question of the Sermon's sources has been examined in this debate. For example, in his summary of the Two-Source Hypothesis, Joseph Fitzmyer notes that one factor in favor of the Two-Source Hypothesis is that it accounts for the presence of the Sermon in Matthew and its absence from Mark. Matthew includes it because he knows the "Q" source which was unknown to Mark.[7] Critics argue that the Griesbach-Farmer hypothesis cannot satisfactorily explain why Mark should omit the Sermon if he knew Matthew.[8]

The Two-Source Hypothesis has retained its dominant position because even while conceding that it has weaknesses, many argue that it is the best explanation currently available. Fitzmyer is typical when he writes:

> Conceivably, the most recent attempts to solve the Synoptic problem might be on the right track or might be more

valid than the Two-Source Theory. However I find them deficient in so many details—some of which I have pointed out above—and raising as many problems as the ones they sought to resolve. Until a more convincing way is found to present one or the other of them, I find myself still attracted to the Two-Source Theory.[9]

The Sources of the Sermon on the Mount

Most specialists working on the Sermon in the last thirty years have used some form of the Two-Source Hypothesis to identify the Sermon's sources and to investigate how Matthew shaped or redacted those sources in constructing the Sermon. Since only a few verses in the Sermon have possible parallels in Mark,[10] scholars have suggested that Matthew redacted two sources in creating the Sermon: i) "Q" the major source and ii) "M," material unique to Matthew. Implicit in this work is the question of how much of the Sermon derives directly or indirectly from the historical Jesus.

Q: A Sayings Source[11]

About 62 of the 106 verses which comprise Matthew's Sermon (5:3–7:27) are similar to verses in Luke's gospel, especially in Luke 6:20–49.[12] For many scholars, at least three factors indicate that this material which Matthew and Luke share comes from the source "Q." i) The material has a considerable number of similar words; ii) while it occurs in different contexts throughout Matthew and Luke, it often appears in the same order; iii) the material is of a similar kind, namely sayings of Jesus.[13]

But while many scholars agree that Matthew has used "Q," they disagree on aspects of that use. We will consider two different discussions of Matthew's use of "Q."

In *The Setting of the Sermon on the Mount*, W. D. Davies discusses Matthew's use of "Q" in general terms.[14] As do many others, he dates the origin of "Q" to the decade of the 50's in Palestine or Syria. His discussion emphasizes i) the proclamatory nature of "Q" and ii) the continuity between the content and function of "Q" and Jesus. For Davies "Q" is not primarily a source which regulates and exhorts Christian living. It is not a catechism,[15] but out of reverence for Jesus' own words, it proclaims what Jesus proclaimed (385). It is a source not of regulation but of radical demand and revelation which points the reader/hearer to Jesus. Matthew's Sermon continues the function of "Q." It requires the reader "to ask who he is who utters these words" (435).

Robert Guelich's consideration of how Matthew uses "Q" is very detailed and specific.[16] He pays attention, for example, to the addition or removal of particular words or verses, to the order in which sayings are combined, to how sayings are introduced and finished, to what parts of the source may have been omitted. Through these changes, he seeks to discover Matthew's distinctive theology or understanding of the significance of Jesus and what it means to follow him. Guelich's approach is representative of much work on the Sermon in recent years.[17]

By comparing the order and content of Luke and Matthew, Guelich argues (as do most others) that Luke's Sermon on the Plain (Lk 6:20–49) is closer to the "Q" Sermon than Matthew's. In Guelich's reconstruction, the "Q" Sermon consisted of three major sections:

i)   a series of beatitudes (Lk 6:20–23);[18]
ii) a series of admonitions (Lk 6:27–45);
iii) the concluding warning in parable form (Lk 6:46–49).

Matthew retains this order except for Lk 6:31 which is moved to Matt 7:12 (see Guelich's summary on the next page). Matthew omits Luke's woes (Lk 6:24–26) and employs two other "Q" sayings from elsewhere in Luke's gospel (Lk 6:39–40; Mt 15:14; 10:24). Matthew also expands the "Q" sermon considerably. He introduces additional material from other parts of "Q," from another source or from his own creation.

Some examples from Guelich's detailed analysis of the beatitudes (5:3–12) will suggest the flavor of his work. Guelich argues that Matthew receives a unit of four beatitudes from "Q" (Lk 6:20b–23), to which in a separate tradition ("Qmt," a form of "Q" known to Matthew but not to Luke) four more had already been added (Mt 5:5, 7–9; Guelich, 113–115). To these eight, Guelich argues, Matthew adds a ninth (5:10). This is a Matthean creation because it uses language and content that Matthew introduces elsewhere ("kingdom of heaven," "righteousness").

Guelich also sees Matthew making significant changes to the *wording* of the "Q" beatitudes. In the first beatitude, Matthew replaces "poor" with "poor in spirit." Guelich interprets this change as Matthew's attempt to broaden the beatitude's focus from socio-economic conditions to include a religious attitude of standing before God as one's only hope (75). Matthew intensifies the fourth beatitude (5:6) by adding a verb ("thirst"). For Guelich, the addition of the important Matthean word "righteousness" changes its focus from material and physical needs to express a more comprehensive relationship with God (116).

Guelich also notices that Matthew reorganizes the *order* of the first three beatitudes drawn from "Q." The third one in "Q" becomes the second one in Matthew. Guelich attributes this change to Matthew's desire to reshape the beatitudes to be in line with Isaiah 61:1–3 (80). This reshaping

TABLE OF PARALLELS

	MATTHEW		LUKE
Q	5:1–2	*Introduction*	6:20a
Q	5:3–12	*Beatitudes*	6:20b–23
	5:13–16		
Q	5:13		14:34–35
	5:14, cf. Gos Thom 1:33		
Q	5:15		11:33
	5:16		
	5:17–20		
	5:17		
Q	5:18		16:17
	5:19		
	5:20		
	5:21–48		
	5:21–24		
Q	5:25–26		12:57–59
	5:27–28		
	5:29–30, cf. 18:8–9, par. Mk 9:43–48		
Q	5:31–32		16:18
	5:33–37, cf. James 5:12		
Q	5:38–42	*Love Your Enemies*	6:29–30
Q	5:43–48	*Love Your Enemies*	6:27–28, 31–36
	6:1–18		
	6:1–8		
Q	6:9–13		11:2–4
	6:14–15, par. Mark 11:25(26)		
	6:16–18		
	6:19–7:12		
Q	6:19–21		12:33–34
Q	6:21–23		11:34–36
Q	6:24		16:13
Q	6:25–34		12:22–32
Q	7:1–5	*On Judging*	6:37–43
	7:6		
Q	7:7–11		11:9–13
Q	7:12	*Golden Rule*	6:31
	7:13–27		
Q	7:13–14		13:23–24
	7:15		
Q	7:16–20, cf. 12:33–35	*On Fruits*	6:34–45
Q	7:21	*Lord, Lord*	6:46
Q	7:22–23		13:25–27
Q	7:24–27	*Two Builders*	6:47–49
	7:28–29		
Q	7:28	*Conclusion*	7:1
	7:29, par. Mark 1:22		

(from Guelich, *Sermon on the Mount,* 34).

expresses Matthew's theological understanding that Jesus fulfills the promises of that passage (98). Guelich sees further examples of the influence of Isaiah 61 on the promise of the third beatitude to "inherit the earth" (83) and in the use of "righteousness" in the fourth (5:6) and eighth beatitudes (5:10; cf. Isa 61:3, 10, 11; Guelich, 87). Guelich argues that Matthew omits the "woes" which follow the four beatitudes in "Q" (Lk 6:24–26) to maintain his focus on the new situation of blessing which God has brought about in Jesus.

Guelich carries out this precise work throughout his commentary. He notices, for instance, that in the concluding section (7:13–27), Matthew combines "Q" material which appears in two different contexts in Luke, chapters 6 and 13.[19] Matthew's redaction provides a conclusion for the Sermon which underlines obedience to Jesus' words and warns about the consequences of the judgment. Christological, eschatological, ecclesiological and ethical dimensions reinforce each other (383–85, 411–13).

Guelich's detailed discussion of "Q" as a source for the Sermon clearly differs from Davies' more general approach. Yet while it might seem that Guelich's attention focuses on the changes that Matthew makes to the tradition, he repeatedly emphasizes that Matthew's changes remain consistent with "the Jesus of the tradition." Matthew clarifies, amplifies and expands the tradition, rather than distorting it (118, 271, 383, 412–13). Like Davies, Guelich insists that Matthew's redaction continues the Christological focus of the tradition (174, 411–413).

Not all scholars agree with all the details of Guelich's analysis of Matthew's redactional work on "Q." For example, Guelich notices that with the beatitudes Matthew changes "Q"'s second person address ("you") to a third person form. He concludes that the change of person is of no account (76). Another redaction critic, Robert Gundry, however, argues that the change is very significant. He interprets it to represent Matthew's intention to make the statements more didactic and to conform them to the dominant Hebrew Bible form. Matthew's change assimilates Jesus' words to the Word of God in the Old Testament.[20]

Though agreeing with Guelich's analysis of the sources of the beatitudes, W. D. Davies and Dale Allison reject his claim that Matthew has redacted the beatitudes under the influence of Isa 61, claiming that this influence on 5:3, 4 and 6 derives from Jesus.[21] Jan Lambrecht and Christopher Tuckett dispute the claim that the beatitudes of 5:5, 7–9 came from "Qmt," preferring to see them as Matthean creations like verse 10.[22]

More radical is Hans-Theo Wrege's claim that the disagreements between Matthew and Luke are so extensive in the beatitudes as to indicate that they did not share a common source at all.[23] George Buchanan, who rejects the Two-Source Hypothesis, notices a unity in the language, content and style of the beatitudes and concludes that all of them were composed by Matthew under the influence of Psalms 24, 37 and 73 and Second Isaiah (Isa 40–55) and not "in any jigsaw fashion, based on hypothetical nonbiblical sources."[24]

A number of scholars disagree with Guelich's claim that Matthew's redaction of the beatitudes continues and intensifies the tradition's sense of Jesus as the fulfillment of the Old Testament and Jesus' followers as the new people of promise in relationship with God.[25] Ulrich Luz sees the pre-Matthean tradition, as well as Matthew's redaction, creating "a shift in the meaning of the Beatitudes in the direction of parenesis" (232). For Luz, the beatitudes become in Matthew's hands "ethicized" as a "catalogue of virtues" and internalized as religious virtues which, nevertheless, also continue to express God's grace as they did in the ministry of Jesus.[26] Lambrecht and Georg Strecker even dispute the preservation of grace and see Matthew's redaction of the beatitudes as establishing requirements to be met before one can enter the kingdom.[27]

Such disagreements are to be expected and could be documented for the discussions of other sections of the Sermon. They remind us that redaction criticism is not an objective, but a subjective, activity. Not only is it complicated by the uncertainty about the exact text of "Q," but it also involves interpreting the changes. Since scholars cannot ask Matthew what he was doing and why, they have to make informed guesses about his intention and meaning. Nevertheless, Guelich's work demonstrates the careful work that has been undertaken to ascertain how the author of Matthew's gospel may have used his main source "Q" in order to express his own theological understanding and to address the situation of his community of followers of Jesus.

M: Matthew's Special Material

We have noticed that Guelich and other scholars refer to material in the Sermon as deriving from "Q" and from a form of Q known only to Matthew ("Qmt") but not to Luke.[28] Some scholars prefer to think of material which does not come from Mark or from the form of "Q" known to Matthew *and* Luke as belonging to a separate source called "M." Burton H. Streeter argues that "M" was a coherent document from the Jerusalem church written in the 60's.[29] It advocates obeying the law and the tradition of the scribes, and has an anti-Gentile bias. In Streeter's reconstruction, there are 48 verses from "M" in the Sermon.[30] Thomas W. Manson and G. D. Kilpatrick also regard "M" as a written source consisting of the material particular to Matthew.[31]

Davies also identifies "M" as a further source for the Sermon. Unlike "Q" 's revelatory function and continuation of Jesus' radical words, Davies sees "M" being "regulatory" in nature, offering guidelines for everyday living. It developed when the expected return of Jesus did not take place and churches settled in for the long haul. It also reflects confrontation with the synagogue as the teaching of Jesus is related to the Jewish scriptures and turned into a new law (5:21ff). The effect of including "M" material alongside the radical "Q" material in the Sermon is to create both proclamation and instruction, revelation and regulation, grace and demand within the Sermon (387–401, 433–35).

In seeking to reconstruct "M," Stephenson Brooks challenges Streeter's methods and conclusions.[32] He argues that it is inadequate to constitute "M" as the material that does not derive from "Q" or Mark for this approach does not take account of material that Matthew contributes. Tradition and redaction must be carefully separated in the unparalleled material in order to constitute "M." Brooks carries out such a separation on the basis of internal tensions (aporias) and inconsistencies, and distinctive style, vocabulary, grammar and content (11–23). Brooks uncovers 9 "M" sayings (consisting of 24 verses) in the Sermon,[33] concluding that they do not derive from a coherent written source or from one geographical or temporal setting (chapters 2 and 6) as Streeter, Manson, Kilpatrick and Davies had argued.[34] Rather, the sayings reflect at least three stages in the Matthean community's relationship with a Jewish synagogue (chapters 5–7), a time of peace (6:1–6, 16–18), of tension (5:23–24; 6:7–8; 7:6), and of independent existence (5:19, 21–22, 27–28, 33–35, 37).

Davies and Allison also reject Streeter's proposal of a unified, written document because the material lacks the necessary literary or theological cohesiveness, and the theory underestimates the extent of Matthean redaction in this material. They list 50 verses in the Sermon as not being from "Q" and attribute 20 of these to Matthew. Of the remaining 30

verses, 4 derive from "Qmt." They suggest that "M" be regarded as a "convenient symbol" for the material that does
not derive from "Q," Mark or Matthew, but which derives
from a variety of possible sources which cannot be recon-
structed with any precision.

For instance, Davies and Allison follow Hans Dieter
Betz in designating 6:1–6, 16–18 as a pre-Matthean "cult-
didache" or teaching for Christians into which Matthew has
inserted the Lord's Prayer (reworked from "Q").[35] With
chapter 23, this source may have helped Christians distinguish themselves from synagogues (Davies and Allison, 126–
27). Another source may have been the three sayings of
similar construction which now comprise 5:21–37. Beyond
this, any evidence is too fragmentary to allow further sources
to be identified. "M" represents not a coherent collection or
document but a diverse assortment of material (125–27).

Jesus

How much of Matthew's Sermon derives from Jesus is
a widely debated question. The debate takes place within a
two-century-long quest for the historical Jesus. During this
time a spectrum of conclusions has been established, rang-
ing from those who say that we can know almost nothing of
the words or voice of Jesus of Nazareth, to those who claim
that the gospels present accurately and fully not just the
voice of Jesus but the very words of Jesus. Scholars have
debated the relationship between historical knowledge and
faith, considered the nature of the gospels (history? biogra-
phy? proclamation?) and investigated how Jesus might have
fitted into first-century Palestine. They have also tried to
assess how conservative or creative the early Christian communities and gospel writers were in passing on and/or in
reshaping and adding to the words of Jesus. In the course of

this debate, a number of criteria have been suggested to assist scholars in identifying the words and actions of Jesus.[36] This, briefly, is the larger context for the investigation of Jesus as a source for the Sermon.

We have already seen in the discussion of "Q" and "M" some diversity in the assessment of Jesus as a source. Both Davies and Guelich generally want to emphasize continuity between the Sermon and its sources, including Jesus. While the Sermon expands the tradition, it preserves its essential content and function deriving from Jesus.[37] S. Agouridès makes an even more direct claim that Matthew's Sermon and Luke's Sermon on the Plain (Lk 6:20–49) derive from sermons Jesus preached on different occasions.[38]

Other scholars doubt that there is as much continuity as Davies and Guelich suggest. We have noted Luz's assessment of the beatitudes (231–32). The three beatitudes that derived from Jesus (unredacted forms of 5:3, 4, 6) expressed "the unconditional, categorical bestowal of grace on people who are in a desperate situation" but through their tradition and redaction by Matthew they have become more ethical statements requiring a way of living (called parenesis; so also Strecker and Lambrecht).[39]

The most extensive investigation of Jesus as a source for the Sermon has been carried out recently by the *Jesus Seminar*. This seminar, sponsored by Polebridge Press and consisting of 30 "Fellows" as well as "Corresponding Fellows," has met regularly since 1985. Its goal has been to make an inventory of sayings attributed to Jesus and to evaluate them according to those that can be attributed to Jesus, those that derive from the early communities and those about which there is uncertainty.[40]

The Seminar has conducted its work through the presentation of papers and extensive discussion. Taking a clue from "red-letter" Bibles, members have then expressed their evaluation of sayings attributed to Jesus by voting. A "red" vote indicates that in the scholar's view Jesus unequivocally said this or something like it and the item should be included in a data base for determining who Jesus was. "Pink" expresses more uncertainty, but indicates the conclusion (with reservations) that Jesus probably said something like this. "Gray" denotes the conclusion that Jesus did not say this and the item should not be included in the data base. However, some of its content may be useful for determining who Jesus was. "Black" indicates that Jesus did not say this item, that it should not be in the data base, and that it represents a later tradition.[41]

The Seminar's work has made several significant contributions to the assessment of Jesus as a source for the Sermon. First, it has emphasized the question of method, of how scholars investigate the historical Jesus. In addition to the criteria developed by historical criticism, the Seminar has been particularly sensitive to the rhetorical structure, nature and function of the language of the tradition.[42]

Second, it has made available its discussion and results for public and scholarly attention. In 1990, it published a full record of its voting.[43] The Sermon was discussed and voted on in a series of 100 units. Some units consisted of a clause from a verse while others consisted of 2 or 3 verses. Of the 100 units, the majority of Seminar members designated 5 units red, 25 pink, 30 gray, and 40 black.[44] They have deemed 70 of the 100 units (gray and black) as probably not deriving from Jesus, while 30 units (red and pink) have been transmitted as accurate or probably accurate reflections of his voice. In the "red" group are 5:39b, 40, 41, 42a, 44b while the beatitudes of 5:3, 4, and 6 are voted "pink." The beatitudes of 5:5, 7–9 are voted "black."[45] The Lord's Prayer was voted on twice. As a whole unit, it received a gray vote indicating that the Seminar does not regard it as a formulation from Jesus. It was also voted on in 9 separate units with 5 receiving pink votes, 3 black votes and one gray.[46]

Also significant is the Seminar's analysis of sources for the Sermon material. The voting table designates 68 units as "Q" material (including 26 units *also* transmitted from the Gospel of Thomas), 37 from "M," with 6 from Mark, 2 from the Dialogue of the Savior, and 1 from the Didache.[47]

The Seminar's results support the position outlined above that "Q" and "M" (however the latter is defined) are the dominant sources for the Sermon. The designation of about a third of the material as being from Jesus (30 of 100 units) supports those who argue that the pre-gospel communities were creative contributors to the growing traditions from and about Jesus.

Alternative Approaches to the Question of Sources

Our focus has been on the sources of the Sermon as identified by the Two-Source Hypothesis. But while most major contributions to the discussion of the Sermon since 1960 have adopted this approach, there are several exceptions which offer alternatives to this dominant view and to the Griesbach-Farmer proposal. We will briefly note three.

1. W. F. Albright and C. S. Mann

One alternative is proposed by W. F. Albright and C. S. Mann in their commentary on Matthew in the Anchor Bible Series.[48] They do not find the Two-Source Hypothesis persuasive. In fact, they doubt whether there is any direct literary relationship among the synoptic gospels and suggest that an original Aramaic or Hebrew gospel offers a better explanation for the similarities among the gospels.[49] This approach has received little support.[50]

2. Hans Dieter Betz

In a series of articles written over a number of years, Betz has argued that

> [T]he SM as found in Matthew's Gospel is a presynoptic source that has been preserved in its entirety. In our view this source does not derive from Jesus of Nazareth directly, but from Jewish-Christian groups residing in Jerusalem sometime around the middle of the first century A.D. The author (there may have been several) drew his material from the tradition of Jesus' sayings and . . . created a compendium of the teaching of Jesus. . . . In its function as an epitome, the SM served to instruct the members of the above-mentioned Jewish-Christian community.[51]

In proposing that the Sermon existed as a completed unit before being incorporated into Matthew's gospel, Betz does not want to do away with "Q." In fact he argues that the Sermon draws from "Q" but the material has been redacted by the pre-Matthean author (103). However, the Sermon is not to be confused with "Q."

In an evaluation article, Charles Carlston raises a number of questions about Betz's understanding of the Sermon as a distinct pre-gospel source which Matthew has incorporated into the gospel.[52] In Carlston's view, the extensive similarities between Matthew and Luke indicate that it is simply not possible to side-step "Q" in this way. Further, Betz's suggestion that the Sermon drew material from "Q" does not leave sufficient time for "Q" and the Sermon source to diverge so significantly in transmission.[53]

Graham Stanton finds other aspects of Betz's analysis unconvincing.[54] Betz's designation of the Sermon as an epitome does not recognize that the Sermon contains only a part of Jesus' teaching. His claim that the Sermon is critical of Paul relies on dubious exegesis of several key verses (5:17; 7:15–23) and fails to explain why such a conservative Jewish group would be persecuted. Finally, similarities between the language, style and theology (Christology and ecclesiology) of the Sermon and the gospel render unlikely Betz's claim that the Sermon was an independent pre-Matthean source.

3. Structural and Literary Approaches

In his 1976 commentary on Matthew, Herman Waetjen, while not ignoring sources, advocated attention to the overall literary shape of the gospel.[55] He sees the Sermon as the first of five discourses placed within the narrative sequence. The alternating pattern of discourse and narrative forms an "integrated composition" and "comprehensive unity." Waetjen's discussion focuses on this finished form.

As another example of an alternative approach, Daniel Patte's commentary on Matthew's gospel can be mentioned.[56] His structuralist approach works primarily with the finished form of the gospel. Issues of origin and sources are not important for this method. He examines the impact of the finished form of the text on readers, paying particular attention to oppositions and tensions in the text.

Conclusion

In this chapter we have asked the question, "Where did the Sermon come from?" We have seen that most scholars answer that question within the framework of the Two-Source Hypothesis, the dominant source "Q" and the smaller collection of sources "M." Matthew forms material transmitted by the early Christian communities and conveying the voice of

Jesus into the Sermon as he composes his gospel. We have also briefly considered some alternative approaches to the question of sources.

But this discussion of sources raises further questions. How has Matthew structured this material? For whom was it written and why? And what is the content or message that Matthew wants to convey to his audience through this carefully shaped material? These questions will concern us in the next four chapters. In the next chapter, we will look at how Matthew has organized or structured this material in composing the Sermon.

Notes

1. See Senior, *What Are They Saying About Matthew?* chapter 1; also chapter 3 below.

2. I retain the traditional name for the gospel author without affirming a particular identity or gender.

3. For discussion, see Arthur J. Bellinzoni, "Introduction" in *The Two-Source Hypothesis* (ed. Arthur J. Bellinzoni; Macon: Mercer University, 1985) 3–19, esp. 14–19; Stanton, *Gospel*, 28–41; for classic statements of the hypothesis, see Bellinzoni's collection, and G. M. Styler, "The Priority of Mark," in Charles Francis Digby Moule, *The Birth of the New Testament* (3d. ed., London: Adam and Charles Black, 1981) 285–316; Werner Georg Kümmel, *Introduction to the New Testament* (Nashville: Abingdon, 1973) 38–80; Joseph A. Fitzmyer, "The Priority of Mark and the "Q" Source in Luke," in *Jesus and Man's Hope* (ed. Donald Miller; Perspective: Pittsburgh Theological Seminary, 1970) Vol. I, 131–170.

4. Burton Hillman Streeter, *The Four Gospels* (New York: Macmillan, 1925) 150–294.

5. For example, Styler, "Priority," 285; Willi Marxsen, *Introduction to the New Testament* (Philadelphia: Fortress, 1968) 118; Stanton, *Gospel*, 51.

6. William Farmer, *The Synoptic Problem: A Critical Analysis* (New York: Macmillan, 1964); B. C. Butler, *The Originality of St Matthew* (Cambridge University, 1951), see chapter 3 for discussion of the Sermon. For review, "The Synoptic Problem: After Ten Years," *Perkins School of Theology Journal* 28 (1975) 63–88, for discussion by Reginald Fuller, Ed Sanders, and Thomas Longstaff.

7. Fitzmyer, "The Priority of Mark," *Jesus and Man's Hope*, 135.

8. This criticism has been answered by supporters of the Griesbach hypothesis. David Dungan ("Mark—The Abridgement of Matthew and Luke," in *Jesus and Man's Hope*, 51–97, esp. 93–97) discusses the nature of Mark's conflation in relation to other reworkings of the gospels in the early centuries of the church. See also William Farmer, "Modern Developments of Griesbach's Hypothesis," *NTS* 23 (1977) 283–93, esp. 285–86.

9. Fitzmyer, "The Priority of Mark," in *Jesus and Man's Hope*, 162. Farmer replies to Fitzmyer in "A Response to Joseph Fitzmyer's Defense of the "Two-Document" Hypothesis," in *New Synoptic Studies* 501–523; see also Farmer, "Modern Developments," 283–93. Extracts from Fitzmyer's article are reprinted in Bellinzoni, *Two-Source Hypothesis*, 37–52, 245–57.

10. Possible parallels include Mt 5:13 with Mk 9:50, Mt 5:15 with Mk 4:21, Mt 5:29–30 with Mk 9:43–47 and Mt 18:8–9, 5:31–32 with Mk 10:11 and 19:9, Mt 6:14–15 with Mk 11:25, and Mt 7:2 with Mk 4:24. Whether Mark knew Q is a debated question.

11. For some classic contributions to the debate about the existence, extent, genre, content and composition of "Q," see Bellinzoni, *Two-Source Hypothesis*, 219–433. Also see the contributions in *Semeia* 55 (1991); John Kloppenberg, Marvin Meyer, Stephen Patterson and Michael Steinhauser, *Q Thomas Reader* (Sonoma: Polebridge, 1990) "Introduction," 3–30; John S. Kloppenberg, *The Formation of Q* (Philadelphia: Fortress, 1987) Chapters 1–3; Howard Biggs, "The Q Debate since 1955," *Themelios* 6 (1981) 18–28. Also Petros Vassiliades, "The

Nature and Extent of the Q Document," *NovT* 20 (1978) 49–73; John Kloppenberg, "Tradition and Redaction in the Synoptic Sayings Source," *CBQ* 46 (1984) 34–62. Studies of the theology of "Q" include Ivan Havener, *Q: The Sayings of Jesus* (Wilmington: Michael Glazier, 1987); Athanasius Polag, *Die Christologie der Logienquelle* (WMANT 45; Neukirchen: Neukirchener, 1977); Richard Edwards, *A Theology of Q* (Philadelphia: Fortress, 1976); for discussion of Matthew's use of "Q" in the Sermon, Syreeni, *Making of the Sermon*, 132–67.

12. This is my count from Polag's text of "Q" in Havener, *Q: The Sayings of Jesus*, 123–146, and from the "minimal" and "generally accepted" text of "Q" constituted by John Kloppenberg, *Q Parallels* (Sonoma: Polebridge, 1988) 2–203. For Kloppenberg's explanation, see p. xxiii.

13. Some want to argue for Luke's use of Matthew as an alternative explanation. See Bellinzoni, *Two-Source Hypothesis*, 321–433.

14. Davies, *Setting of the Sermon*, 366–86. For a shortened version, Davies, *The Sermon on the Mount* (Cambridge: Cambridge University, 1966) 101–108.

15. This was the consensus of earlier scholars of "Q." So Adolf von Harnack, *The Sayings of Jesus: The Second Source of St. Matthew and St. Luke* (London: Williams and Norgate; New York: G. P. Putnam's Sons, 1908); Martin Dibelius, *From Tradition to Gospel* (New York: Charles Scribner's Sons, 1935); Vincent Taylor, *The Formation of the Gospel Tradition* (2d ed., London: Macmillan, 1935); Thomas W. Manson, *The Sayings of Jesus* (London: SCM, 1949).

16. Robert Guelich, *The Sermon on the Mount: A Foundation for Understanding* (Dallas: Word, 1982).

17. Among recent commentaries, see, for example, Daniel Harrington, *The Gospel of Matthew* (Sacra Pagina 1; Collegeville: Liturgical, 1991); W. D. Davies and Dale Allison, *The Gospel*

According to Saint Matthew Vols. 1 and 2 (ICC; Edinburgh: T. & T. Clark, 1988, 1991); Ulrich Luz, *Matthew 1–7* (Minneapolis: Augsburg, 1989); also Georg Strecker, *The Sermon on the Mount* (Nashville: Abingdon, 1988); Jan Lambrecht, *The Sermon on the Mount: Proclamation and Exhortation* (Good News Studies 14; Wilmington: Michael Glazier, 1985); Herman Hendrickx, *The Sermon on the Mount* (London: Geoffrey Chapman, 1984); Robert Gundry, *Matthew: A Commentary on His Literary and Theological Art* (Grand Rapids: Eerdmans, 1982); Eduard Schweizer, *The Good News According to Matthew* (Atlanta: John Knox, 1975).

18. It should be noted that scholars debate the origin and context of the beatitude form. For discussion see Guelich, *Sermon*, 63–66.

19. Luke 6:43–44 parallels Matt 7:16–20, Lk 6:46 parallels 7:21 and Lk 6:47–49 parallels 7:24–27. This material is reinforced by the addition of "Q" material which Luke uses in chapter 13. Matthew 7:13–14 draws from Lk 13:23–24, and 7:22–23 from Lk 13:26–27.

20. Gundry (*Matthew*, 67–68) generally agrees with Guelich's analysis.

21. Davies and Allison, *Matthew I*, 436–39; their agreement with Guelich that 5:3–4, 6, 11–12 derive from "Q," 5:5, 7, 8, 9 from "Qmt," and 5:10 from Matthew is evident on 434–436. Also in agreement with this analysis are Luz, *Matthew*, 227–29; Strecker, *Sermon*, 29–30; Hendrickx, *Sermon*, 16–18; Schweizer, *Good News*, 82–86.

22. Lambrecht, *Sermon on the Mount*, 60–62; Christopher M. Tuckett, "The Beatitudes: A Source-Critical Study," *NovT* 25 (1983) 193–207, esp. 200–202.

23. Hans-Theo Wrege, *Die Überlieferungsgeschichte der Bergpredigt* (WUNT 9; Tübingen: J. C. B. Mohr, 1968) 5–27.

24. George W. Buchanan, "Matthaean Beatitudes and Traditional Promises," in *New Synoptic Studies* (ed. William Farmer; Macon: Mercer University, 1983) 161–84, esp. 180.

25. Guelich, *Sermon*, 108–118.

26. Luz, *Matthew 1–7*, 243–46. Strecker (*Sermon*, 29–47) also stresses the ethical orientation of the beatitudes.

27. For instance, Strecker, *Sermon*, 33; Lambrecht, *Sermon*, 62–64.

28. Guelich, *Sermon*, 115; Stanton, *Gospel*, 287; Luz, *Matthew*, 48–49; Strecker, *Sermon*, 11–13; Lambrecht, *Sermon*, 37–39; Hendrickx, *Sermon*, 3–5.

29. Streeter, *Four Gospels*, 150, 232.

30. Streeter (*Four Gospels*, 198) identifies within 5:3–7:27 these "M" verses: 5:4–5, 7–10, 13a, 14, 16–17, 19–24, 27–28, 31–39a, 41, 43; 6:1–8, 10b, 13b, 16–18, 34; 7:6, 12b, 15, 19.

31. Thomas W. Manson, *The Teachings of Jesus* (2nd ed., London: Cambridge University, 1939) 21–44, esp. 34–38; *Sayings of Jesus* 21–26; G. D. Kilpatrick, *The Origins of the Gospel according to St. Matthew* (London: Oxford University, 1946) 8–36. In the Sermon, Manson (*Sayings*, 23) attributes the following to "M" (parentheses indicate doubt): 5:7–10, (13–16), 17–24, 27–39a, 43, (44a), (44b–48); 6:1–4, 5–8, (9–15), 16–18, 34; 7:6, 13–14, 15, (16–20), 21–23. Kilpatrick (*Origins*, 35) attributes: 5:19–20, 21–24 (in part), 27–28, 33–37, 38–41 (in part); 6:1–8, 16–18.

32. Stephenson Humphries Brooks, *Matthew's Community: The Evidence of His Special Sayings Material* (Sheffield: Sheffield Academic, 1987).

33. Brooks (*Matthew's Community*, chapter 2, 91–93, 160–62) lists 5:19, 21–22, 23–24, 27–28, 33–35 and 37a–b, 36; 6:1–6 and 16–18, 7–8; 7:6.

34. Brooks (*Matthew's Community*, chapters 2–4; summary 160–62) identifies 19 "M" units in 5:17–6:18 and chapters 10 and 23 consisting of 48 verses. This is not all of "M"; he allows for further "M" material in the parables which he does not examine.

35. Davies and Allison, *Matthew I*, 126, 573–75. Hans Dieter Betz, "A Jewish-Christian Cultic Didache in Matt. 6:1–18: Reflections and Questions on the Problem of the Historical Jesus," in Hans Dieter Betz, *Essays on the Sermon on the Mount* (Philadelphia: Fortress, 1985) 55–69. David Hill (*The Gospel of Matthew* [NCB; Grand Rapids/London: Eerdmans, Marshall Morgan & Scott, 1972] 31–34) is close to Davies and Allison. In addition to "Qmt," Strecker (*Sermon*, 14) refers to "isolated special material" (oral traditions) but does not designate it "M."

36. Daniel Harrington ("The Jewishness of Jesus: Facing Some Problems," *CBQ* 49 [1987] 1–13, esp. 9–10) identifies four criteria. (1) A gospel saying must reflect the conditions of Palestine in Jesus' time and/or be capable of translation back into Aramaic or Hebrew. (2) It should be found in several independent early Christian strands of tradition. (3) It must be coherent or consistent with what is known about Jesus. (4) It must be so unique that it cannot be ascribed to Judaism or to the early church. Georg Strecker (*The Sermon on the Mount* [Nashville: Abingdon, 1988] 13) identifies three: a saying does not derive (1) from Judaism, (2) from the post-Easter community; (3) remove the redactional additions to sayings. See also M. Eugene Boring, "The Historical-Critical Method's 'Criteria of Authenticity': The Beatitudes in Q and Thomas as a Test Case," *Semeia* 44 (1988) 9–44, esp. 12–24; Robert Stein, "The 'Criteria' for Authenticity," *Gospel Perspectives* vol. I (eds. Richard France and David Wenham; Sheffield: JSOT, 1980) 225–63.

37. Davies, *Setting of the Sermon*, 415–35; also, Lambrecht, *Sermon*, 39–40.

38. S. Agouridès, "La Tradition des Béatitudes chez Matthieu et Luc," in *Mélanges bibliques en honneur au R. P. Beda Rigaux* (eds. A. Descamps et al.; Gembloux: Duculot, 1970) 9–27.

39. A similar disagreement exists over 5:21–48. Guelich wants to locate these antitheses in the ministry of Jesus to "the sick, the sinner and the righteous" (271, 259–60), while also recognizing their considerable development in the tradition and by Matthew's redaction (256–71). On the other hand, Luz regards four of the antitheses (nos. 3–6) as being formed by Matthew (though including some material from Jesus), while only the first two antitheses derive from Jesus (5:21–22, 27–28), and are expanded by tradition and redaction. M. Jack Suggs ("The Antitheses as Redactional Products," in *Essays on the Love Commandment* [ed. Reginald H. Fuller; Philadelphia: Fortress, 1978] 93–107) argues that the form derives from Matthew.

40. See the opening remarks of its Chairperson at the 1985 meeting. Robert W. Funk, "The Issues of Jesus," *Foundations and Facets Forum* 1 No. 1 (March, 1985) 7–12; also Robert W. Funk, "Form and Function," *Foundations and Facets Forum* 1 No. 1 (March, 1985) 51–57.

41. In this summary, I have conflated the two options set out in Robert W. Funk, "Poll on the Parables," *Foundations and Facets Forum* Vol. 2 No. 1 (March, 1986) 54–80, esp. 54–55.

42. As one example, Robert W. Funk, "Unraveling the Jesus Tradition: Criteria and Criticism," *Foundations and Facets Forum* 5.2 (June, 1989) 31–62, esp. 33.

43. "The Jesus Seminar Voting Records," *Foundations and Facets Forum* 6,1 (March, 1990) 3–55.

44. By my count 13 units were discussed and voted on twice on separate occasions. Seven repeat votings produced the same result, while 6 lead to different results. Of these 6, 4 show a trend toward doubt in the voting sequence while one (7:3–5)

shows the reverse trend. The sixth, 5:34b–37, were three votes on different aspects of the unit.

45. The periodical *Foundations and Facets Forum* (available from Polebridge Press) contains a number of the articles on the SM discussed by the Seminar, as well as reports of those discussions.

46. See the report of the discussion and voting in Robert J. Miller, "The Lord's Prayer and Other Items from the Sermon on the Mount," *Foundations and Facets Forum* 5.2 (June 1989) 177–86, esp. 179–83. See also the important paper by Hal Taussig, "The Lord's Prayer," *Foundations and Facets Forum* 4.4 (Dec 1988) 25–41. Most commentators on the Sermon (Luz, Davies and Allison, Strecker, Lambrecht, Hendrickx, Guelich, Schweizer, Gundry, Hill) recognize it as a prayer taught by Jesus though influenced by the liturgical practices and traditions of their congregations. Michael Goulder, *Midrash and Lection in Matthew* (London: SPCK, 1974), p. 298, finds it to be composed by Matthew.

47. Space precludes discussion of these other possible sources, just as it also precludes discussion of possible connections with the Pauline traditions, or with the book of James (see Peter Davids, *The Epistle of James* (Grand Rapids: Eerdmans, 1982) 15–16, 47–51.

48. W. F. Albright and C. S. Mann, *Matthew* (Anchor Bible 26; Garden City, New York: Doubleday, 1971) xxxvii–liii.

49. Jeremias (*Sermon on the Mount*, 13–23) offers a somewhat similar analysis. He does not mention "Q," and argues that the isolated sayings of the Sermon material were originally gathered into an Aramaic, then Greek collection. The Sermon existed as a catechism for baptismal candidates or newly baptized Christians.

50. For critique, Robin Scroggs, "A New Old Quest? A Review Essay," *JAAR* 40 (1972) 506–12.

51. Hans Dieter Betz, "Cosmogony and Ethics in the Sermon on the Mount," *Essays on the Sermon on the Mount*, 89–123, esp. 90.

52. Charles Carlston, "Betz on the Sermon on the Mount," *CBQ* 50 (1988) 47–57.

53. Carlston has other difficulties. i) Betz suggests that the Sermon was a philosophical epitome of Jesus' teaching. But Carlston comments that even if this Jewish-Christian community knew this form (which he doubts), it is still not a convincing designation since Betz does not demonstrate *formal* similarities between this genre and the Sermon. ii) Carlston is not persuaded by the history of early Christianity in which Betz wants to locate the pre-Matthean Sermon in fights against "*Gentile* Charismatics of a 'Pauline stamp' " (52). iii) Betz's lack of concern with any Matthean redactional activity in the Sermon is unconvincing. iv) Betz's statement of the Christology of the Sermon (Jesus is a teacher and eschatological judge) is understated. v) Carlston does not agree with Betz's view that the language and theology of the Sermon are radically different from Matthew's Gospel. He points to at least five points of similarity (56).

54. Stanton, *Gospel*, 309–25. Dale Allison ("A New Approach to the Sermon on the Mount," *Eph Th L* 64 [1988] 405–414) also finds Betz's approach unconvincing. He disputes Betz's claim of i) the pre-Matthean origin of Mt 5–7, ii) the Sermon's conscious engagement with Hellenistic philosophy, iii) the Sermon as a systematic and comprehensive presentation of the theology of Jesus for a community that was not interested in the passion or resurrection of Jesus.

55. Waetjen, *Origin and Destiny*, 15–25.

56. Daniel Patte, *The Gospel According to Matthew: A Structural Commentary on Matthew's Faith* (Philadelphia: Fortress, 1987).

2
The Structure of the Sermon on the Mount

In this chapter, our focus moves from the sources which Matthew used in writing the Sermon to its structure. How have scholars understood the structure or shape of the final form of the Sermon? How did Matthew organize the material from the various sources into a unified whole? These questions build on our investigation of sources. They also impact our understanding of the Sermon's function (chapter 3) and content (chapters 4 and 5).

Scholars have suggested a variety of ways of understanding the structure of the Sermon. I will discuss six approaches.

1. The Beatitudes as the Basis of the Sermon

In his 1974 book, *Midrash and Lection in Matthew*, Michael Goulder suggests that the eight beatitudes of 5:3–10 provide the structure for the Sermon.[1] Goulder argues that Matthew does not derive these beatitudes from the source "Q" but creates them in rabbinic style to form the *kelal*,[2] a summary of, or heading for, the Sermon. Like the list of covenant blessings in Deuteronomy 27–28, they announce the blessing of the new law, revealing who is truly blessed. Then in the rest of the Sermon, these eight blessings are expounded in reverse order by means of triple illustration, also a familiar rabbinic practice (251–54).

For example, 5:11–16 elaborates the eighth beatitude from 5:10. Verses 11–12 provide the first example of persecution (verbal abuse), and define the nature of blessedness as reward in heaven. The saying about salt (5:13) continues the persecution theme by naming salvation through suffering as a fundamental reality. The saying about light in 5:14–16 adds a third aspect. Goulder understands "light" to be a reference to the gospel whose proclamation results in martyrdom (254–55). The three-fold expansion of the beatitude of 5:10 in 5:11–16 is followed by a transition passage (5:17–20). The next section (5:21–26) provides a threefold elaboration of the seventh beatitude, the blessing on peacemakers (5:9). Then follows the elaboration of the sixth beatitude, the pure in heart (5:8), in 5:27–37.

In summary form, what Goulder's understanding of the structure of the Sermon looks like can be found in the chart on p. 37.

Goulder's discussion of Matthew's gospel and the Sermon is detailed and stimulating. He draws attention to some aspects that are not often addressed and insists on the unity of the Sermon. But his analysis has generally been rejected. As our discussion in the last chapter indicates, most scholars do not find convincing any attempt to dispense with "Q" and "M" as sources. Most prefer to retain "Q" as an explanation for the similarities and differences in the material common to Matthew and Luke, rather than follow Goulder in positing Luke's use of Matthew.[3]

A further difficulty with Goulder's analysis is that it

THE UNITY OF THE SERMON

Beatitudes cf. Pentecost.

(8) Persecuted	(a) Reward in heaven	5:11–12
	(b) Salt of earth	5:13
	(c) Light of cosmos	5:14–16
	Law and Prophets fulfilled	
(7) Peacemakers	(a) No anger, rudeness, insult	5:21–2
	(b) Reconciliation	5:23–4
	(c) Come to terms	5:25–6
(6) Pure in heart	(a) No lust (heart/eyes/hands)	5:27–30
	(b) No remarriage	5:31–2
	(c) No false oaths (Ps.24.6)	5:33–7
(5) Merciful	(a) No *talio*	5:38–42
	(b) No hatred	5:43–8
	(c) No parade in "mercy"	6:1–4
(4) Hunger and Thirst for Righteousness	(a) No parade in prayer	6:5–8
	(b) Lord's Prayer	6:9–15
	(c) No parade in fasting	6:16–18
(3) Meek (Ps. 37.11)	(a) Treasure in heaven	6:19–21
	(b) Generous eye	6:22–4
	(c) No anxiety	6:25–34
(2) Mourners	(a) No judging	7:1–2
	(b) No reproving	7:3–5
	(c) No backbiting	7:6
(1) Poor in spirit	(a) Ask, seek, knock	7:7–11
	Law and Prophets in a Kelal	7:12
Peroration	(a) Two Gates, Two Ways	7:13–14
	(b) False Prophets. Two Trees and Fruits	7:15–23
	(c) Two Builders	7:24–7

(from Goulder, *Midrash and Lection in Matthew,* 269).

ignores some of the Sermon's more obvious subdivisions. Davies and Allison are unhappy with the separation of the ninth beatitude (5:11–12) from the first eight in 5:3–10 (430). It is equally difficult to accept Goulder's destruction of the unity of the antitheses in 5:21–48 by proposing 5:38–6:4 as the elaboration on the fifth beatitude on mercy (5:7).[4]

This proposal also destroys the unity of 6:1–18. For example, Guelich names 6:1 as a *kelal* or heading for 6:1–18 in which verses 2–18 expand the principle announced in verse 1. The word in 6:1 (translated in RSV and NRSV as "piety") is the same word as is translated "righteousness" in 5:20. The repetition of this key word in 6:1 indicates to him that 6:1–18 elaborates the "greater righteousness" demanded in 5:20 and already developed in 5:21–48 (273, 275). Goulder's structure does not recognize this link.

There are also problems with the lack of integration of 5:17–20. Goulder styles this section as the introduction of the "second theme," the fulfillment of the law, which is developed through the rest of chapter 5 (256, chapter 13). Immediately apparent is that 5:17–20 interrupts the careful elaboration of the eight beatitudes begun in 5:11–16. On Goulder's reading, this elaboration is halted awkwardly at 5:17–20 only to be resumed at 5:21.

Further, how this second theme is connected to the first theme is not clear. Goulder argues that 7:12 is a summary of the theme of the fulfillment of the law and the prophets introduced in 5:17–20 (268). On Goulder's reading, 7 of the 8 beatitudes and their elaboration are devoted to the second theme. The place of the first theme, the eighth beatitude and its elaboration (5:10–16), is not articulated.

Goulder's claim that the beatitudes provide the Sermon's structure produces some strange sequences and units. His argument that the theme of persecution links 5:11–12 and 5:13–16 reduces the rich diversity of the salt and light images and arbitrarily highlights one dimension. That 7:1–6 forms a unit to elaborate "mourning" is not convincing. Neither is his reading of 7:6 in relation to backbiting. At heart, Goulder's creative proposal faces the central problem of the lack of explicit verbal clues and repetitions in the text which would guide readers to the connections with the beatitudes that he proposes.

2. Patte's Chiastic Structure

Another proposal which sees considerable literary sophistication and patterning in the Sermon comes from Patte's commentary on Matthew. Patte argues that the Sermon is structured as a *chiasm*. A chiasm is a

> reverse parallelism. Two or more terms, phrases or ideas are stated and then repeated in reverse order. . . . [Its] critical characteristics [are] *balance* and *inversion* as well as focus on the *central verse or verses* as the important turning point in the events.[5]

These features are demonstrated in Patte's outline:[6]

A1–5:3–10. Beatitudes. Who the disciples are.
   B1–5:11–16. The disciples' vocation.
      C1–5:17–19. Conditions for implementing the vocation.
         D1–5:20. Introduction of antitheses (framing material)
            E1–5:21–47. Antitheses. The overabundant righteousness.
         D2–5:47–48. Conclusion of antitheses (framing material)

D3 – 6:1. Introduction to next unit (framing material).

E2 – 6:2–18. The overabundant righteousness.

D4 – 6:19–21. Conclusion of preceding unit (framing material)

C2 – 6:22–7:12. Conditions for implementing the vocation.

B2 – 7:13–20. The disciples' vocation.

A1 – 7:21–27. Who the disciples are.

Patte identifies a narrative framework around the Sermon (5:1–2; 7:28–29) which, he argues, underlines its nature as authoritative teaching. The overall task of the Sermon is to have readers accept it as authoritative teaching which they should obey. Each section contributes to this goal. The "A" material plays a special role in establishing an "I-thou" relationship between Jesus and the readers/hearers which enables them to accept the teaching as authoritative. The initial "A" section, the beatitudes, invites readers/hearers to become disciples, to join the blessed. The final "A" section (7:21–27) brings the Sermon back to the issue of the readers/hearers' acceptance of the teaching and provides the key characteristic of balance for the structure.

The "B" material expresses the vocation to which readers/hearers are called. The "C" material identifies some conditions for implementing the vocation: correct understanding of scripture (5:17–19), and having a life characterized by the overabundant righteousness described in 5:20–6:21 (6:22–7:12). The "D" material points to different kinds of righteousness, to opposite ways of fulfilling a vocation. The central "E" material outlines what disciples are to do if they are to enter the kingdom. The first section (5:21–47) describes "abundant righteousness" in relation to other people, while the second section (6:2–18) describes it in relation to God (60–105).

Patte's suggestion has several positive features. His outline recognizes righteousness as central to the Sermon, a concern shared by a number of scholars (see section 5 below). The center of his chiasm holds together the two large teaching blocks of 5:21–47 and 6:2–18 and underlines their related yet different contributions to defining the "abundant righteousness" demanded in 5:20. His focus on the nature of discipleship is also well placed.

But the outline is not without its weaknesses. Patte's concern to find balance and correspondence forces some unconvincing analysis of both content and structure. In the "A" material, for instance, the designation of the beatitudes as invitations to the readers/hearers to join the blessed does not do justice to the beatitude form as a declaration about an existing situation.[7] Nor does this claim about their function take into account the context of the Sermon in Matthew's gospel. Readers/hearers have already witnessed disciples responding to Jesus' call (4:18–22). Moreover, 5:1–2 carefully differentiate disciples from the crowds so that Jesus addresses *disciples* at the outset of the Sermon (however one interprets 7:28–29).

Other designations and divisions are also problematic. The separation of 5:3–10 from 5:11–12 is unconvincing, as we observed with Goulder's approach. It is difficult to see the appropriateness of Patte's designation for 5:17–19 and 6:22–7:12 as "conditions for implementing the vocation." For most commentators these sections supply further instruction about the life of discipleship which disciples are to lead. The separation of 5:17–19 from 5:20 and 6:22 from 6:19–21 is also generally unsupported by commentators. While most commentators see 6:22–23 as a subunit after 6:19–21, there is no support for the idea that 6:22 initiates a larger new section. Also unconvincing is the designation of 6:19–21 (D4) as a concluding frame for the previous section (6:2–18). 6:19–21 introduces new content which is developed in 6:22–24.

3. The Lord's Prayer as the Center:
   Luz, Bornkamm, Guelich

Somewhat similar to Patte's analysis is Luz's proposal that the Lord's Prayer provides the basis for the structure of the Sermon. Luz is, though, more interested in the effect of movement through the sections than finding the exact correspondences of function and content which marked Patte's outline.

Luz sees a series of ringlike structures which frame the Lord's Prayer and narrow the focus to 6:9–13 (212). The first ring or frame is formed by 4:23 and 9:35 which draw the Sermon together with chapters 8–9 to present the "Messiah of Word (5–7) and Deed (8–9)."[8] The second frame is created by 4:25–5:2 and 7:28–8:1. These units, drawn together by several repeated terms ("crowds," "follow") lead into and out of the Sermon. The third frame consists of the Introduction to the Sermon (5:3–16) and the Conclusion (7:13–27), both of which emphasize the "kingdom of heaven" (5:3, 10; 7:21) and the doing of Jesus' teaching. The fourth frame moves toward the central teaching block, providing an Introit (5:17–20) and Conclusion (7:12). The shared phrase "the law and the prophets" connects these units and names the doing of God's will as the theme of the central section (216–217). The main section embraces 5:21–7:11 and divides into three units. Luz identifies the antitheses of 5:21–48 and the section on possessions, judging and prayer in

6:19–7:11 as the frame, both consisting of 59 lines in the Greek text. Bracketed by these sections is 6:1–18. Within it, 6:1–6 and 6:16–18 provide the frame for the center of the Sermon, the Lord's Prayer in 6:7–15.

One of the strengths of Luz's suggestion is its contribution to understanding the content of the Sermon. He argues that the structure highlights a fundamental dimension of the discipleship demanded by the Sermon. The function of the material up until 6:6 - the ethicized beatitudes (5:3–12), the demand for greater righteousness (5:20), the antitheses which illustrate perfection (5:21–48) – is to lead readers through action to prayer, through God's demanding will to the place of encounter with God's grace. God's grace enables disciples to live God's will which the material after 6:15 continues to announce (215, 388–89, 454). A subsequent section on prayer (7:7–11) will reinforce this central inter-relationship of action and prayer (424).

Luz's proposal to find the Lord's Prayer at the center of the Sermon is not a new one. Other scholars have also noticed its central location.[9] What is significant is the way in which Luz has drawn important theological understandings from this analysis of the Sermon's structure. His proposal is a strong one and it remains to be seen how much support it will receive from scholars.[10]

At least one aspect, though, will not be convincing for some. Luz divides the section 6:19–7:11 into two subunits, 6:19–34 which focuses on possessions, and 7:1–11 which addresses various questions (390–91). Three factors suggest that this proposal is not adequate. i) To label 6:19–34 "Possessions" does not recognize its diversity. 6:22–23 does not easily belong and the new focus on "anxiety" at 6:25 is not indicated. ii) Luz recognizes but does not give weight to the fourfold use of negative commands through the section

(6:19, 25; 7:1, 6). iii) His analysis does not elucidate how the disparate material within 6:19–7:12 forms a coherent unit.

3b. The Lord's Prayer and 6:19–7:12: Bornkamm

Many scholars have struggled to find unity in the apparently loose collection of material found in 6:19–7:11.[11] In an important article, Günther Bornkamm argues that 6:19–7:11 is an elaboration of the Lord's Prayer.[12] 6:19–24 develops the concern of the first three petitions of the Lord's Prayer (6:9b–10) with the priorities and central focus of disciples. 6:25–34 expands the fourth petition's emphasis on the provision of material needs (6:11). 7:1–5 unpacks the implications of the prayer for forgiveness (6:12) in relation to a community that is free from judgment. 7:6 elaborates the sixth and seventh petitions (6:13) for deliverance from evil in a life of faithfulness, not apostasy. 7:7–11 provides assurance that prayer is indeed heard and answered in daily living. 7:12 concludes both this section and the larger unit from 5:17.

Bornkamm's proposal has several merits. It offers a rationale for Matthew's redaction of apparently diverse "Q" material in this section. Further, his analysis recognizes the four negative commands (6:19, 25; 7:1, 6) as markers which indicate the beginning of new sections. It also explains the presence of the concluding unit on prayer (7:7–11). The opening *positive* command of 7:7 continues the function of commands as section markers, while also drawing attention to the reassuring content of this section.

Bornkamm's analysis has been supported by Guelich (324–25) and Stanton,[13] and, with qualifications, by Lambrecht (155–64). But it has not received universal approval.[14] Lambrecht is not convinced that 7:1–5 develops the prayer's concern with forgiveness. Davies and Allison agree with

Lambrecht's assessment that Bornkamm's proposed connection between 7:6 and the sixth and seventh petitions on the basis of apostasy is "somewhat farfetched." Luz does not find the interpretation of 6:19–24 in relation to the first three petitions to be "plausible" (390, note 2). He regards any connection between the petition for forgiveness and 7:1–5 as too general to be significant. The attempt to link 6:13 and 7:6 "restricts both texts too much" (390). Davies and Allison prefer to see a different thematic unity through the section. In 6:19–34 the issue of how to treat wealth is dealt with and in 7:1–12 how to treat one's neighbor. Holding the two sections together is concern with "social issues," "life in the temporal, 'secular' world" (627).

Nevertheless, Bornkamm's suggestion does offer some commendable features, not the least of which is its reading of 6:19–7:12 as a coherent section concerned with prayer, and as an integral part of the Sermon.

4. Conflict with First-Century Religious Leaders and the Synagogue

In the next chapter I consider the question of what particular circumstances Matthew was addressing in forming the Sermon. One leading explanation is that he was addressing a situation in which his community had recently separated from a synagogue and was now establishing its own identity. Not surprisingly, a number of scholars have seen the structure of the Sermon shaped by this context.

For example, Joachim Jeremias sees this dispute as determining the structure of the central section of the Sermon. After the introduction (5:3–19) and thematic sentence (5:20), the dispute between Jesus and the theologians over the interpretation of scripture controls 5:21–48. The controversy with the righteousness of the Pharisees shapes 6:1–18, and a new righteousness for disciples of Jesus is explicated in 6:19–7:27.[15]

In a recent article, Dale Allison also argues along these lines. A simplified outline of the main divisions of his detailed proposal is as follows:

> Nine Beatitudes for the people of God: 5:3–12
> The task of the people of God in the world: 5:13–7:12
>   Jesus and the Torah: 5:17–48
>   The Christian Cult: 6:1–18
>   Social Issues: 6:19–7:12
> Concluding statements and warnings: 7:13–27

He argues that the Sermon is influenced by debates within post-70 Judaism about how faith, life and worship could be conducted now that the temple is destroyed. Matthew fashions a document from the Jesus tradition "to establish the Christian version of what matters most" (442–45).

One of the leading factors for Allison in pointing to this conclusion is a factor that Goulder had also identified, the importance of triads in the Sermon's structure. Even in the simplified outline above, one can see a basic three-part structure which contains a further three-part subdivision (5:17–7:12). But within each of these divisions, Allison finds additional triadic patterns. For example, the six antitheses of 5:21–48 divide into 2 groups of triads (5:21–32; 33–48). The unit of 7:1–6 divides into three further subunits, 7:1–2, 3–5, 6.

Allison argues that this pattern of triads derives from a classic Jewish formulation used to express the wisdom of revered teachers. One teacher in particular, Simeon the Just, is said to have declared that the world stands on three things,

Torah, temple and deeds of loving-kindness (442–43). Employing a pattern of triads in the Sermon indicates, for Allison, Matthew's attempt to show Jesus presenting how the world is to be among his disciples.

Allison's analysis helpfully underlines the connection between the Sermon and the context in which it was written. But in places his preoccupation with triads seems forced. For example, his summary highlights that there are nine beatitudes but his discussion (429–31) does not justify why a 3×3 analysis of the unit is any more justifiable than a 4 + 5 or 4 + 4 + 1 configuration. And, in Betz's view, there are 10 beatitudes, not nine, an observation that for Betz signals the Sermon's concern with perfection.[16]

In parts of Allison's analysis, groups of "two" also figure prominently. The initial summary statement about the task of the people of God consists of two images (5:13–16), there are 2 groups of antitheses (5:21–48), a subdivision of 2 exists within 6:5–15, the major section 6:19–7:12 subdivides into 2 units. There is even a section which highlights two ways (7:13–14) and two house builders (7:24–27). Yet Allison's analysis attributes no significance to this aspect of the structure.

A sense of special pleading is also present in his discussion of the departure from a triadic structure. He highlights two places where the triadic pattern is absent (6:25–34, 7:7–11) and concludes that this departure is intentional to offer encouragement to the reader in the midst of a bombardment of uncompromising demands (435–36). While there is no dispute that these sections offer encouragement, that function may have more to do with the content and the imperatival style than with the absence of a triadic pattern.

Nevertheless, Allison's comprehensive analysis helpfully highlights both the larger and smaller structures of the Sermon. He also makes an important contribution in connecting this structure to the context addressed by the Sermon.

5. Thematic or Theological Organization

Other scholars see a central theme or theological content determining the Sermon's structure.

Guelich seeks to discover the Sermon's structure from its "pivotal concepts and phrases, the thematically related material, and the underlying framework of the Sermon tradition" (37). What holds the Sermon together for Guelich is its theological coherence. The beatitudes provide a Christological and eschatological foundation by declaring the blessings that result from God's promised kingdom present already in part in Jesus. 5:13–16 underlines the eschatological nature of the present expressed in faithful discipleship. Ecclesiology and ethics are immediately emphasized as corollaries of God's action in Jesus.

The heart of the Sermon (5:17–7:12) is concerned with "greater righteousness." The demands of this life are Christologically grounded in the fulfillment of the Old Testament scriptures in Jesus. This new relationship with God is expressed in the lifestyle of the community of disciples. 5:21–48 outlines righteousness with reference to others, while 6:1–7:11 depicts righteousness in relation to God (worship, 6:1–18; a life of prayer, 6:19–7:11). The concluding warnings focus the alternatives of responding negatively or positively to Jesus' ministry (36–39).

Several theological concepts control Guelich's analysis. Its Christological basis in Jesus as the fulfillment of God's promises in the Old Testament tradition is central. The eschatological nature of the present (as well as of the future) is also underlined. So too are the ecclesiological and ethical implications of God's action in Jesus. Two terms are central for his analysis, "kingdom of heaven" whose blessings are presented in the beatitudes, and "righteousness" which describes a new relationship with God and the way of life or discipleship that it produces. Guelich entitles 5:3–16 "The Blessings of the Kingdom," and 5:17–7:12 "The Greater Righteousness" (39).

Jack Kingsbury proposes a somewhat similar analysis.[17] Kingsbury is not, though, concerned with the impact of the tradition as is the redaction critic Guelich. As a literary critic, Kingsbury is more concerned with the finished form of the text which "implied readers" receive. The "implied reader" is identified in the gospel (24:15; 27:8; 28:15) as a disciple of Jesus after the resurrection (135–36). The Sermon is, for Kingsbury as for Guelich, teaching for disciples predicated on Jesus' identity as the Son of God in whom God's kingdom is present (134).

The center of this teaching is the theme of "greater righteousness" announced in 5:20. This term sums up

> the style of life intended to be the mark of disciples of Jesus . . . the quality of life which is indicative of disciples who make up the church. It is behavior which comports itself with living in the sphere of God's kingdom. . . . In sum therefore, it is love toward God and love toward neighbor that constitute the heart of the greater righteousness. (136–37)

Kingsbury sees the five sections of the Sermon explicating this style of life of the "greater righteousness" (136).

(1) Introduction: On Those Who Practice the Greater Righteousness (5:3–16)
(2) On Practicing the Greater Righteousness Toward the Neighbor (5:17–48)

(3) On Practicing the Greater Righteousness Before
      God (6:1–18)
(4) On Practicing the Greater Righteousness in Other
      Areas of Life (6:19–7:12)
(5) Conclusion: Injunctions on Practicing the Greater
      Righteousness (7:13–27)

Similarities with Guelich's analysis in both divisions and theological emphases are immediately apparent. The theme of "greater righteousness" controls the outline. This "greater righteousness" results from and centers on the gospel's Christology. A new situation is created in the present by the kingdom of heaven, by eschatological salvation in Jesus (138). This new reality creates a way of life lived in the community of disciples, that is in the church, "the new community of God's eschatological people" (138). Ecclesiology and ethics derive from the Christological and eschatological starting points.

Both analyses have the merit of explicating the larger structure of the Sermon without seeking to determine a very detailed outline for the smaller units. We have seen that some detailed proposals are led into unrealistically artificial constructions. Both scholars also present outlines which carefully reflect the larger didactic function of the Sermon.[18]

Other themes have been suggested by scholars. Olav Hanssen argues that the commandment to love God and neighbor provides the theme.[19] Within this theme, he draws attention to the Sermon's concern with relationship to the world and the task of mission. His analysis reflects a tension between universality and particularity in the Sermon. 5:3–16 addresses the nature and task of the community of Jesus; 5:17–7:12 is concerned with "better righteousness" but Hanssen sees it being developed in two sections and directions. 5:21–6:18 is concerned with Christianity's relationship to Judaism (5:21–48, the new relationship with one's neighbor; 6:1–18, the new relationship with God). 6:19–7:12 is concerned with the relationship between the Christian community and the Gentile world with the two divisions (6:19–34; 7:1–12) addressing the same two issues but in reverse order. The four sections within 5:21–7:12 are thus drawn together by a chiastic structure.

Christoph Burchard proposes that "the will of God" provides the determining theme.[20] Mission and love form important components of this theme; 5:16 is the key verse. The Introduction (5:3–16) summarizes the contents (64, 73), while the Body of the Sermon (5:17–7:12) explains in two sections how to carry out this task of living "good works" (64, 73–74). In 5:17–48, the will of God is asserted while 6:1–7:12 offers guidelines for its fulfillment (73). A Conclusion (7:13–27) warns disciples against failure to fulfill this commission (74–75).

6. General Outlines

Some proposals identify considerable literary skill in the structure of the Sermon. Some offer very detailed analyses which reflect their understanding of the function, circumstances and theological content of the Sermon. In this section, we will note that some scholars propose more general outlines. These outlines are often not discussed and do not seem to be shaped by distinctive historical and/or theological factors. They tend to highlight what could be regarded as "commonsense" divisions like 5:17–20, 5:21–48, and 6:1–18.[21]

Lambrecht's outline offers a good example.[22] The Sermon comprises a prologue (5:3–16), a middle (5:17–7:12) and an epilogue (7:13–27). The middle section divides into three: "the antitheses" (5:17–48), "not before men" (6:1–18), and "unconcern and commitment" (6:19–7:12).[23]

These approaches have the advantage of being straight-forward outlines of the larger (and usually non-controversial) divisions of the Sermon. They are also essentially free of the overstretching evident in some of the approaches discussed above. They often lack, however, the close attention to the historical and theological specificity of the Sermon and to its unity which influences other approaches.

Conclusion

From this discussion, we can note several conclusions. First, there is significant diversity in analyses of the structure of the Sermon. While most scholars generally agree on some key markers and units (5:17, 5:21; 6:1), there is no consensus around one overall analysis or on particular subunits. Even these possible points of consensus have their detractors as we have noted. Second, we have seen some scholars attempt complex analyses while others are content to offer general outlines. The more sophisticated readings emphasize de-tailed divisions, consistent patterns, interaction and balance between sections. The more general outlines are content to identify several main sections and markers but without press-ing the analysis. This diversity reflects how subjective and individualistic is the act of interpreting a text. Third, we have observed the importance for several analyses of a scholar's understanding of the function of the Sermon. Understand-ings of function which are connected to specific socio-historical circumstances or theological themes significantly influence the scholar's analysis of the shape of the Sermon.

It is to the question of the Sermon's function for the particular socio-historical circumstances of its readers that we turn in chapter 3.

Notes

1. Michael Goulder, *Midrash and Lection in Matthew.* Austin Farrer (*St. Matthew and St. Mark* [Westminster: Dacre, 1954] ch 10) had earlier proposed that the Sermon was Matthew's composition (176) based on the beatitudes. Betz ("The Beatitudes of the Sermon on the Mount [Matt. 5:3–12]: Observations on their Literary Form and Theological Significance," in *Essays*, 17–36) argues that "the rest of the Sermon is nothing else than the concretization and elucidation of the first macarism [beatitude]" (35).

2. For Goulder's discussion of *kelal* as a general summary from which specific examples can be drawn, and as one of Hillel's principles of interpreting scripture, see *Midrash*, 20, 25.

3. See the literature in Bellinzoni, *Two-Source Hypothesis.*

4. Davies and Allison, *Matthew*, 560. Luz (*Matthew 1–7*, 338) names its function as a *kelal* for 5:21–48; Hill, *Gospel of Matthew*, 131; Gundry, *Matthew*, 99–100; Guelich, *Sermon*, 255.

5. James L. Bailey and Lyle vander Broek, *Literary Forms in the New Testament: A Handbook* (Louisville: Westminster/John Knox, 1992) 49, 178–79.

6. Patte, *Matthew*, 65.

7. Among others, Betz ("Beatitudes," 26–35) emphasizes that the beatitudes convey knowledge concerning the present in relation to the future.

8. Luz (*Matthew 1–7*, 203) quotes from J. Schniewind, *Das Evangelium nach Matthäus* (8th ed., NTD 2. Göttingen: Vandenhoeck and Ruprecht, 1956) 36.

9. Schweizer (*Good News*, 202–03) briefly suggests some connection between the structure of the Sermon and the Lord's Prayer but does not demonstrate it in detail. He comments

only that "the first three petitions are developed in the sections that precede, the last three in the sections that follow (6:19–34; 7:1–12, 13–23)." Also Hendrickx, *Sermon*, 108, 128–29; Walter Grundmann, *Das Evangelium nach Matthäus* (THKNT 1; 3d ed.; Berlin: Evangelische Verlaganstalt, 1972) 204–06; Farrer, *St. Matthew*, 169–76.

10. Luz's claim that the Lord's Prayer lies at the center of the Sermon also receives support from Jack Dean Kingsbury ("The Place, Structure and Meaning of the Sermon on the Mount Within Matthew," *Interpretation* 41 [1987] 131–143). However, he does not adopt Luz's structure. See further below. Stanton (*Gospel*, 298) finds the correspondence between 5:21–48 and 6:19–7:11 to be forced.

11. For example, Strecker (*Sermon*, 130) comments that Matthew joins "sayings of various content" from "Q"; David Hill ("The Meaning of the Sermon on the Mount in Matthew's Gospel," *IBS* 6 [1984] 120–33) calls 6:19–7:27 a "series of loosely related sayings"; Hendrickx (*Sermon*, 149) says that 7:1–12 "groups together a number of sayings without much logical or real relationship"; Lambrecht (*Sermon*, 151) notes that the previous concern with order seems to disappear in this section.

12. Günther Bornkamm, "Der Aufbau der Bergpredigt," *NTS* 24 (1977–78) 419–32.

13. Stanton, *Gospel*, 298.

14. Davies and Allison, *Matthew*, 676, note 19; Lambrecht, *Sermon*, 164. For a more sustained critique, see Dale Allison, "The Structure of the Sermon on the Mount," *JBL* 106 (1987) 423–45, esp. 424–29.

15. Joachim Jeremias, *The Sermon on the Mount* (FBBS; Philadelphia: Fortress, 1963) 22–23.

16. Betz, "Beatitudes," 23.

17. Kingsbury, "Place, Structure and Meaning," 131–43.

18. Several other analyses are driven by the concept of "righteousness." Neil McEleney ("The Principles of the Sermon on the Mount," *CBQ* 41 [1979] 552–70) argues that 5:17 introduces the main section of the Sermon entitled "Program of Christian Action" (5:17–7:12). 5:17–20 provides the structural principles for this section, fulfilling the law and greater righteousness. 5:21–48 outlines fulfilling the law in contrast to the righteousness of the Pharisees, while 6:1–7:12 develops the greater righteousness further. Hill ("Meaning of the Sermon," 122–23, 128) proposes a structure that is very much akin to the outlines of both Jeremias (see above) and McEleney. 5:21–48 shows what "more-than-scribal" righteousness looks like; 6:1–18 discloses "better-than-Pharisaic" righteousness, and 6:19–7:12 outlines "disciples-style" righteousness (128).

19. Olav Hanssen, "Zum Verständnis des Bergpredigt," in *Der Ruf Jesu und die Antwort der Gemeinde* (ed. Eduard Lohse; Göttingen: Vandenhoeck & Ruprecht, 1970) 94–111; summary 103–04.

20. Christoph Burchard, "The Theme of the Sermon on the Mount," in *Essays on the Love Commandment* (ed. Reginald H. Fuller; Philadelphia: Fortress, 1978) 57–91.

21. See Schweizer, *Good News*, 79–209; Strecker, *Sermon*, 14–15; Hendrickx, *Sermon*, v–vii; Harrington, *Gospel of Matthew*, 76; Stanton, *Gospel*, 297–98; D. R. A. Hare, *Matthew* (Interpretation; Louisville: John Knox, 1993) 34–87 and Table of Contents.

22. Lambrecht, *Sermon on the Mount*, 26–29; Syreeni (*Making of the Sermon*, 168–206) also adopts a tripartite structure based on the inclusion of 5:17 and 7:12.

23. Jacques Dupont (*Les Béatitudes: Tome I* [2nd ed.; Paris: Gabalda, 1969] 175–82) surveys a number of analyses before proposing (181) a four-part structure consisting of the beatitudes (5:3–12) and three main parts: perfect justice (5:17–48), good works (6:1–18) and three admonitions (7:1–17).

3
The Function and Socio-Historical Setting of Matthew's Sermon on the Mount

In working with his sources (chapter 1) and shaping them into the organized structure of the Sermon (chapter 2), Matthew is a pastoral theologian. He presents the teaching of Jesus so that it addresses and guides his late first-century community of disciples of Jesus. In this chapter I will discuss some of the suggestions made about the situation of the Sermon's audience and about its function for these people.

Clues present in the Sermon and throughout Matthew's gospel provide the primary source of information about this community. As Stanton warns, any attempt to mirror-read the text of the Sermon and the gospel as sources for information about Matthew's readers must be tentative and circular. That is, "in order to read the text responsibly, we need to know about the circumstances that elicited it, but in our quest for its setting we have only the text of the Gospel itself."[1]

Space precludes a discussion of every aspect of this issue. For instance, with regard to the time and location of the community addressed by the Sermon, many scholars place the community in the large Syrian city of Antioch in the 80's of the first century. Other places have been suggested (Jerusalem, Alexandria, Phoenicia, Caesarea Maritima). However, the reference to Syria in 4:24, the likely use of Matthew by Ignatius the bishop of Syria early in the second century, and the significant role given to Peter in the gospel which matches his prominence in the Antiochene church point to Antioch as a likely, though not certain, place of origin. Particularly important for our discussion will be to investigate how scholars have understood the circumstances or experiences of the community being addressed.[2]

Matthew's Community and Post-70 Judaism

Davies suggests that the function of the Sermon must be understood in relation to the situation of Judaism after the destruction of the Jerusalem temple in 70 CE by the Romans.[3] Davies identifies two dangers facing Judaism in this traumatic time. One danger came from divisions within Judaism; the other from forces outside Judaism such as the growing Christian movement. With the disastrous outcome of the war against Rome (66–70 CE), zealots, Sadducees and priests lost their powerful leadership positions. The Pharisees emerged as the leading group because of their flexible theology, their distance from the temple, their influence among people as a lay group, and their concern with all of life as an act of service to God. Under the leadership of Rabbi Yohannan ben Zakkai (and later Gamaliel II), a group of Pharisaic leaders met at the coastal town of Yavneh (also called Jamnia). They asserted their authority to interpret the law, to regulate Jewish life and to order worship in the synagogue.[4]

They also set about preserving Jewish identity from external enemies. These enemies included, in Davies' view, the growing Christian movement as evidenced by Matthew's community. One of the main ways of protecting Jewish identity was the insertion of a curse on heretics (*minim*) into the *Teffilah*, the Eighteen Benedictions recited during worship.[5] Davies thinks the twelfth benediction (or *Birkath ha Minim*) was composed by Samuel the Small around 85 CE and was close to this wording:

> For persecutors let there be no hope, and the dominion
> of arrogance do Thou speedily root out in our days; and
> let Christians and *minim* perish in a moment, let them be
> blotted out of the book of the living and let them not be
> written with the righteous.

The reciting of this curse during synagogue worship made non-participating Christian members conspicuous and effected their removal from the synagogue (275–76).

But not only was "Jamnian Judaism consciously confronting Christianity." Matthew's gospel sets about formulating a distinctive Christian identity and way of life. In the Sermon,[6] Davies sees the beatitudes expressing God's approval for one group of people rather than another. In the blessing on the persecuted (5:11–12), the division and hostility between the persecuted Christian community and the persecuting synagogue is clear. This contrast continues in 5:13–16 and throughout the main teaching section in 5:20–7:12. Explicitly in 5:20 the demands of Jesus are contrasted with those of the Pharisees (286–92). In 6:1–18 the piety of the Christian community is contrasted with the hypocrites in the synagogue (6:2, 5, 16).

Davies also sees the structure of the Sermon as reflecting the confrontation with Jamnia. The sermon's threefold concern with the Torah of Jesus (5:21–48), worship (6:1–18), and loving kindness (6:19–7:12) reflects a post-70 debate. Davies argues that after the fall of the temple, post-70 Judaism had to reinterpret the saying of Simeon the Just that the world is supported by works of Torah, the temple cult and deeds of kindness. The sermon offers Matthew's reinterpretation in which the teaching of Jesus and the practice of prayer have central positions (304–315; see the discussion of Allison's article in the previous chapter).

Davies concludes that the Sermon is

> the Christian answer to Jamnia . . . a kind of Christian, mishnaic counterpart to the formulation taking place there. . . . It was the desire and necessity to present a formulation of the way of the new Israel at a time when the rabbis were engaged in a parallel task for the Old Israel that provided the stimulus for the evangelist to shape the *SM*. (315)

By presenting the teaching of Jesus as central for his community (for example, the focus on Jesus' words in 7:24–27), Matthew seeks to secure its identity and guide its lifestyle in an unsettled time and to counter the claims originating from Yavneh and the synagogue.

While Davies' emphasis on the dispute between Matthew's community and the synagogue has been very influential, aspects of his analysis have not been universally accepted.[7] A number of scholars doubt that it is possible to claim such direct connection between Matthew's Sermon and Yavneh, particularly the *Birkath ha Minim*.[8] For one thing, the reconstructive work carried out at Yavneh took place over many decades and it is not possible to pin down the formulation of any one policy or action to one time. Just when the *Birkath ha Minim* was formulated cannot be determined with any accuracy. Hence its relevancy to the composition of the Sermon is uncertain.

Nor is it clear how "decisions" from Yavneh were disseminated and what authority may have been accorded them in synagogues. Davies' presentation suggests a central controlling body whose power was widely recognized and whose decisions were greeted with universal compliance. But such a scenario seems idealized and does not account for the necessary process of time or the diversity of practice evident in post-70 Judaism. And even if such "official" action took place, it is not clear that the *Birkath* was its vehicle. Scholars have pointed out that the *Birkath* prays that the heretics will be destroyed and blotted out of the book of life by God, rather than excluded from a synagogue community.

Davies' claim that there was a curse directed against Christians is questionable on two further grounds. It is not clear whether the words translated by Davies as "Christians and heretics" in the twelfth blessing (*notzrim* and *minim*) existed in the earlier forms of the statement and whether they referred specifically to Christians. Nor is it clear that Christian groups such as Matthew's posed a major threat to the survival of Judaism. The absence of references to Christian groups in secular writers until the second decade of the second century suggests how unnoticed and inconsequential these groups may have been in the larger society. Further, within the Sermon, the metaphor, "you are the salt of the earth" (5:13), provides an image that, among other things, contrasts a small entity with a huge context. Likewise the designations of the community in chapter 18 as "children" (18:2–5) and "little ones" (18:6, 10, 14) suggest a situation of marginality and powerlessness. Such contrasts may indicate something of the social location and self-perception of Matthew's community.

The analysis of D. Harrington takes account of this critique in offering a significantly modified version of Davies' argument.[9] Like Davies, Harrington understands Matthew's gospel to be "one of several Jewish responses to the destruction of the Jerusalem Temple in A. D. 70" which attempts to reconstitute "Judaism without Temple and land." But while he recognizes that Matthew's gospel is in tension with other rival responses (the early rabbinic movement, apocalyptic groups), Harrington's analysis does not posit the explicit and direct attacks that Davies identifies. Nor does he give any central place to the *Birkath*. Harrington sees the rabbinic responses developing from Yavneh more slowly and gaining authority much later.

Matthew's Community and the Synagogue: Other Perspectives

Within Davies' analysis, there is some lack of clarity about how he conceives of the relationship between the synagogue and Matthew's community. In several places, he suggests that the Sermon reflects a dispute between several groups within a synagogue (an "in-house" or "intra muros" argument),[10] yet elsewhere he suggests that the gospel evidences "a great gulf . . . between the Christian community and the synagogue" (286). His discussion of the *Birkath ha minim* also suggests that he sees a situation in which Christians are excluded from synagogues.

This issue of the relationship between the synagogue and Matthew's community has been extensively debated as scholars have tried to formulate a more precise analysis. Early in the 1960's, Bornkamm argued that the Sermon was written at a time when Matthew's readers were still within Judaism.[11] Bornkamm argues that a central part of the dispute between the two groups was "the right interpretation of the law" (25). The antitheses of 5:21–48 evidence this conflict and the Sermon writer's allegiance to Jesus as the interpreter.

However, in his subsequent work, Bornkamm seems to have changed his mind. He now agrees with the position of most scholars that the Sermon addresses a community that has separated from the synagogue.[12] In a 1970 article, he writes:

> Here [Matthew's] church, although still very small, knows itself to be cut off from the Jewish community; gathered no longer about the Torah but in the name of Jesus, in faith in him and in confession of him, and as such to be assured of his presence.[13]

If Davies' claim that the *Birkath ha minim* effected this separation is perhaps not convincing, what evidence is there that Matthew's community is separated from the synagogue? Scholars have noted a number of features from the gospel. Douglas Hare investigates the theme of Jewish persecution of Christians by drawing attention to the rejection and bitterness evidenced in 5:10–12 as well as 23:29–39, 10:16–37, and 22:6.[14] Because of the rejection of its message about Jesus among the synagogues of Pharisaic Judaism, Matthew's community ceases any mission to Israel (148) and turns toward the Gentile world with the offer of salvation (21:43; 146–66).

In his commentary, Luz also argues that the emphasis on Gentile mission reflects the community's location outside the Jewish synagogue system. This separation from the synagogue is reflected in the use of phrases such as "their" or "your" synagogues and scribes (4:23; 9:35; 12:9; 13:54; 23:34; 7:29), in the typecasting presentation of Jewish leaders and people, and in the absence of any discussion between the synagogue and Matthew's community. The gospel strengthens the self-understanding of the community after the separation (88) and after its recent, probably controversial, decision to engage in Gentile mission. "One of [Matthew's] most important concerns is to defend in his community the decision for the Gentile mission" (84).

The Sermon emphasizes Christian practice for the community as well as providing content for mission proclamation since Jesus commands his disciples to teach the nations all "that I have commanded you" (28:20). The sermon's appeal to the Old Testament (5:17; 7:12) establishes the Old Testament as the

> basis and center of the will of God [which] is deepened and intensified by Jesus' proclamation of the will of God. In the situation where the community and synagogue go separate ways, this programmatic reference back to the law and the prophets means a no toward Israel, for whom Jesus is not the key to the Bible. (214–17)

Though not convinced that mission to Israel has finally ended (276), Stanton also sees the separation as having taken place immediately prior to the writing of the gospel and Sermon.[15] He notes that frequently Matthew strengthens polemic against the synagogue in the traditional material he receives. For example, while the final beatitude drawn from Q names God's blessing on those who are persecuted (5:11), Matthew has intensified this theme by the addition of another beatitude in 5:10. The sharp contrast established in 5:20 between the reader and the "scribes and the Pharisees" as well as in chapter 6 indicates where the persecution originates (267–68). "It is characteristic of sectarian groups to call in question the integrity of the group from which they have separated" (5:20; 6:1–18; *Gospel*, 322). Stanton concludes that Matthew's purpose in strengthening this polemic is not evangelistic (he is not writing for outsiders) but is addressed to the believing community to help it come to terms with the trauma and pain of separation. The intensity of the denunciation of the Jewish leaders (chapter 23 for instance) derives from anger and frustration at being rejected. It reflects the "community's self-justification for its position as a somewhat beleaguered minority "sect" cut off from its roots" (271–74). It can be noted that Stanton's emphasis is close to Guelich's comment that the community's break with the synagogue has "left . . . wounds that were still open and vulnerable" (26).

But for Stanton this community's mission is not just rejected by synagogues but also largely by Gentile society. The references in 5:13 and 14 to being "salt" and "light" indicate a community that perceives itself in mission to but distinct from its surrounding society. The three hostile references to Gentiles in 5:47, 6:7; 32 reflect a sense that the community is "set over against the world at large, and yet it is certainly not cut off from society in general" (277–78). Rejection, alienation and hostility mark this community's societal experience and perception. Using the work of sociologists Wilson and Burridge, Stanton designates the community as a "millenarian sect." The gospel and the Sermon function to explain the community's sense of alienation and to reinforce group solidarity (281–82).

While most scholars have seen the Sermon addressing a community that has recently separated from the synagogue, a few have argued that the dispute with the synagogue belongs further in the community's past.[16] In this view, the Sermon essentially addresses a Gentile community adjusting to its new situation of distance from its Jewish past. In his study of Matthew 5:17–48, J. P. Meier argues that the Gentile author Matthew reinterprets the role of the law (a key part of the community's Jewish heritage) to address the Gentile community.[17] The author's Gentile identity is reflected in several crucial mistakes. Only a Gentile would misunderstand the parallelism of Hebrew poetry and have Jesus ride on two animals at the same time as he enters Jerusalem (21:5). Only a Gentile would betray the ignorance of Jewish institutions evident in 22:23 and 16:11–12 (14–21).

Most scholars, however, do not find this view convincing. The gospel's Jewish flavor and the recent separation from the synagogue offer more satisfying explanations for the difficulties that have been raised.[18] Most see the community addressed by the Sermon as being a predominantly, though not exclusively, Jewish-Christian community, recently separated from the synagogue and open to Gentiles in mission. The Sermon proclaims the definitive and authoritative teaching of Jesus for this community. It provides guidance on how disciples of Jesus are to live and sustains the community's self-understanding in a situation of transition and marginality.

Internal Circumstances

We have concentrated on the relationship of the Sermon to a community in conflict with a synagogue. Other scholars have emphasized the Sermon's address to particular *internal* issues which Matthew's community is experiencing.

Community Identity Legitimation

Waetjen sees the gospel addressing the issue of the community's identity in the difficult post-70 time.[19] Waetjen calls the gospel a "charter document" for a community of predominantly Jewish but also Gentile Christians. It outlines the community's origin, identity, ministry and suffering in relation to Jesus. The charter calls the community to an identity which transcends racial, national, social, and religious tensions and boundaries by its inclusion of Jews and Gentiles, rich and poor.

Betz regards the Sermon as contributing significantly to Matthew's double goals of correcting Mark's presentation of the life of Jesus and of explaining to his readers their church's place in history.[20] The teaching and ministry of Jesus provide the community's "fundamental framework and standard" (270). As a pre-Matthean source, the Sermon is taken into the presentation of the life of Jesus to become part of Jesus' legacy of the "gospel of the kingdom" (4:23), the foundation that Matthew's community is to preserve and interpret in its new situation (270). The new situation includes being a "Christian community that was no longer part of the Jewish religion," no longer obeying Jewish Torah or practicing circumcision, and consisting now of Jews and Gentiles (272). This situation derives from Jesus' "Abrahamic Judaism" which motivated his Gentile mission. The Sermon contains "first inklings" of this mission in its metaphors of light and salt (5:13–16). The Sermon's inclusion in the gospel thus helps to show "the way in which the church gradually developed out of Judaism and became the worldwide Christian community of which [the writer] and his readers are members" (275).

Internal Divisions: The Law

Other interpreters have seen the Sermon addressing various divisions within Matthew's community. In his discussion of "Matthew's Understanding of the Law," Gerhard

Barth sees Matthew disputing not only with opponents out-side his community but also with a group of *antinomians* within his community.[21] In passages such as 5:17–20 and 7:15–23 (also 24:11–13) Barth sees Matthew asserting the abiding validity of the law against this group who argued that Christ's coming meant that the law and prophets were no longer to be followed. Others have identified this group as later followers of Paul,[22] but Barth does not think such a claim to be sustainable. Barth cannot find any evidence that Matthew's opponents base their position on Paul's under-standing of faith; rather from 5:17 he thinks they oppose the law because of the coming of Christ (162). Instead of being concerned with obeying the law as interpreted by Jesus, this group of Hellenistic Christians ("Hellenistic libertines") fo-cuses more on charismatic gifts and doing miracles (7:15–23). Through the Sermon and the gospel, Matthew repeat-edly emphasizes doing God's will, yielding fruit, and the threat of judgment.

Others, though, are not convinced that these verses indi-cate the presence of an antinomian group within Matthew's community. Strecker argues that the phrase which intro-duces 5:17 ("Do not think") states a theoretical possibility only. This is how the same phrase is used in 10:34. Along with a number of scholars, Strecker sees the concern with "lawlessness" in the gospel (the word ἀνομία appears in 7:23; 13:41; 23:28; 24:12) as part of Matthew's general in-struction to the whole community rather than as dealing with a particular group.[23]

Harrington also rejects the suggestion of internal divi-sion. He sees the instructions reflecting the division between Matthew's community, "Jews who accept Jesus' interpreta-tion of Torah," and those outside who do not accept Jesus' authority.[24]

The difficulty in claiming that these references (5:17–20; 7:15–23) refer to a group within the Matthean community that wants to ignore the law is also seen in comparing Barth's interpretation with that offered by Guelich. Guelich sees 5:17–19 not in relation to a group that wants to be free of the law but as deriving from a Jewish-Christian group who wanted to hold to a strict "legalistic" interpretation of the law's commandments and prohibitions.[25] Guelich argues that Matthew's redaction of this traditional material reinterprets the sayings in terms of an eschatological framework, that Jesus brings about what the scriptures promise (136–74). While Matthew's presentation functions to resist tendencies to both legalism and antinomianism (173), Guelich sees Matthew as being more concerned with the presence of Jewish-Christians who advocate a legalistic interpretation (26, 390–411). The vastly differing interpretations offered by Guelich and Barth indicate the difficulty of identifying a particular group in the Matthean community from these sayings.

Further Divisions

In a detailed and stimulating article,[26] Leland White argues that the Sermon is addressed to a community that is experiencing considerable factionalism and inner strife over issues of lifestyle (85). White employs the work of cultural anthropologist Mary Douglas to investigate the sense of *group* (the experience of the bounded social unit) and *grid* (the fit between the values of community members and their everyday reality or social world).

White observes several ways in which the Sermon establishes strong boundaries between those who follow Jesus and those who do not. The antitheses of 5:21–48 urge conformity to socially held values and a strong group identity which seeks to distinguish the community from its society (69–73). They also advocate wary participation in social interaction (5:23–25, 33–37, 39–41). Further, he observes from a number of clues (the lack of formal power structure and recognition of rank, the egalitarian understanding of status and roles, the assumption of hostility and powerlessness in society, the concept of honor and righteousness) that the sense of fit between the community's values and societal experience is low (73–80). The beatitudes, for instance, identify the community's self-understanding as "an ostracized and persecuted faction." Yet the beatitudes also reframe that experience by assigning the community the honor or righteousness of being children of God (81).

White cautiously interprets his findings from the Sermon in the larger context of Douglas' work. Douglas observes that communities with a strong group sense and low grid are frequently subject to factionalism and internal strife. White finds evidence of both aspects in the Sermon in its references to excluding those who do not measure up (5:13; 7:15, 22) and in its scenarios of division and judgment (5:22; 7:15–23). The strong group boundaries not only distinguish the community from outsiders but also provide norms for the behavior of insiders. The provision of such norms of honor and righteousness points to the likely prevalence of evil and shame in the community. The Sermon functions to "define the identity and way of life of Matthew's community among themselves, as well as in reference to their neighbors and God" (87).

White's article, like that of Stanton's, makes an important contribution by its use of a model from cultural anthropology. Significantly, his findings that the community addressed by the Sermon is called to be an egalitarian and alternative community but is not living as faithfully as it might because of division and strife confirm the results of other studies which have reached similar conclusions though by different methods (redaction, literary or historical criticism).[27]

The Sermon and a Community in Transition

Eduard Schweizer has argued that Matthew's gospel and Sermon address a community of itinerant and charismatic prophets.[28] This group moved in the border regions of Galilee and Syria; having renounced family, home and possessions, it wanders from village to village teaching and healing in a lifestyle that imitates Jesus'. The passage 7:15–23 warns the community about its way of life and about being deceived by false prophets within it.[29]

Jack Kingsbury is not convinced by this analysis.[30] He argues that a number of factors—Matthew's Greek, his use of the word "city" but avoidance of "village," his familiarity with a range of money terms, his tempered presentation of Jesus' travels, his concern more with the rich than the poor—indicate the community was domiciled, urban and suspicious of miracle-working (64–72). Matthew's redaction which changes Luke's blessing on "the poor" to a blessing on the "poor in spirit" reflects a community situation very different from Schweizer's itinerant community (67). The warning of 7:15–23 discourages miraculous activity (69–70).

Kingsbury argues that the sayings which advocate abandoning family and possessions had functioned earlier in the tradition to endorse an ethic of "itinerant radicalism." But Matthew's community is now in a "transitional phase" (73) in which most members of the settled urban community do not literally observe this radical teaching, though a few missionary members continue to do so. The sayings concerning forsaking home and possessions now have a "paradigmatic function, setting forth the nature, not necessarily the specifics, of discipleship." They illustrate "the character of discipleship, of being single-heartedly devoted to God" for a community that finds itself in circumstances that differ greatly from that addressed by its traditions (72–73). The gospel and Sermon thus instruct about discipleship in a relatively new situation.

The Sermon and the Worship of the Matthean Community

Michael Goulder sees another internal need shaping the Sermon and being addressed by it. We have noted above Goulder's argument that Matthew creatively expands his only source Mark under the influence of the scriptures to address his particular congregation. Goulder argues that the Sermon, for instance, is composed on the basis of Mark 10, Exodus 19–20:23, some Psalms and chapters from Isaiah.[31]

One of the needs addressed by the Sermon and gospel was the liturgical life of Matthew's congregation.[32] The structure of the gospel follows the Jewish liturgical year, providing readings for the congregation's worship. Jewish festivals are reworked in the light of the Christian traditions about Jesus. The Sermon is the reading for Pentecost, the feast celebrating the giving of the law. In writing the Sermon, Matthew particularly reworks the Exodus 19–20 account of that event read at the Jewish festival of Pentecost. Jesus delivers the Sermon from the mountain (5:1) thereby giving the new law which, in the six antitheses of 5:21–48, is carefully distinguished from the old.[33] The community's worship and life are constituted by the teaching of Jesus.

Two issues have been particularly problematic in Goulder's work. Most scholars are not convinced that we know enough about first-century synagogues and their liturgical and lectionary practices (note the plural) to claim them as the basis for such a thesis. Further, scholars are not persuaded that we know enough about the worship of the early Christian communities like Matthew's to draw the connections Goulder sees or to assume that Christian communities would imitate synagogue practices.[34]

Conclusion

The community addressed by the Sermon was perhaps located in the city of Antioch in Syria in the decade of the 80's in the first century. For most scholars, the strained relationships between this community and the synagogue are an important aspect of its experience (Davies, Bornkamm). Most think it has undergone significant transition in leaving the synagogue (Luz, Hare, Stanton) and in seeking to adjust as disciples to urban and settled existence (Kingsbury). In this context, the Sermon functions to shape its identity and way of life in a new situation which includes mission to a somewhat hostile and rejecting Gentile world (Stanton, White).

Further, the community faces strife within itself over its beliefs (Barth, Guelich) and its way of life (White). The Sermon interprets these experiences in relation to being disciples of Jesus and provides direction, warning and encouragement. Chapters 4 and 5 examine the content which the Sermon presents to its audience.

Notes

1. Graham Stanton, "The Communities of Matthew," *Interpretation* 46 (1992) 379–91; for discussion of some recent contributions and their methods, Jack Dean Kingsbury, "Conclusion: Analysis of a Conversation," in *Social History of the Matthean Community* (ed. David Balch; Minneapolis: Augsburg Fortress, 1991) 259–69.

2. Our discussion will focus as much as possible on the Sermon on the Mount. However, since the Sermon is also part of Matthew's gospel, discussions of the setting and function of the gospel as a whole are relevant. See Senior, *What Are They Saying About Matthew?* chapter 1; Davies and Allison, *Matthew 1–7*, 127–47; Kingsbury, *Matthew as Story*, chapter 9; Balch (ed.), *Social History*. Among recent commentators, Gundry (*Matthew*, 599–609) favors a pre-70 date of around 64–65 CE.

3. Davies, *Setting of the Sermon*, 256. See the discussion in the previous chapter of Allison's article, "Structure of the Sermon"; also Davies and Allison, *Matthew 1–7*, 133–38.

4. Davies, *Setting*, 259–72. See Jacob Neusner, *From Politics to Piety: The Emergence of Pharisaic Judaism* (Englewood Cliffs: Prentice-Hall, 1973).

5. Kilpatrick (*Origins of the Gospel According to St. Matthew*, chapter 6) had earlier emphasized the role of the *Birkath Ha Minim*.

6. Davies' discussion extends beyond the Sermon to include material elsewhere in Matthew's gospel. He notes, for instance, the pervasive hostility toward the Pharisees (16:11–12; 23:1–36), the dispute over the resurrection (28:15), the references to "their" synagogues (4:23; 9:35; 10:17; 12:9; 13:54), the interpretation of Jerusalem as a place of unfaithfulness (22:7) and of Galilee as a place of salvation (28:7, 10, 16). Our discussion will maintain a focus on the Sermon on the Mount.

7. For a rejection of Davies' thesis that the Sermon is a Christian answer to Jamnia, see Georg Strecker's review in *NTS* 13 (1967) 105–112, esp. 107–111; also in the third edition of his *Der Weg der Gerechtigkeit* (Göttingen: Vandenhoeck und Ruprecht, 1971) 257–67; Krister Stendahl, *The School of St. Matthew and its Use of the Old Testament* (2nd. ed.; Philadelphia: Fortress, 1968) xii–xiii; Senior, *What Are They Saying*

about Matthew? 8; Stanton, "Origin and Purpose," 1913; Luz, *Matthew 1–7*, 88; Stanton, *Gospel*, 142–45, 307–08, fn 1. Harrington (*Gospel of Matthew*, 10–16) sets the gospel in relation to post-70 Judaism and in controversy with a synagogue but does not mention Yavneh.

8. Reuven Kimelman, "*Birkat Ha-Minim* and the Lack of Evidence for an Anti-Christian Jewish Prayer in Late Antiquity," *Jewish and Christian Self-Definition*, vol. 2 (eds. E. P. Sanders, Albert I. Baumgarten, Alan Mendelson; Philadelphia: Fortress, 1981) 226–44; Steven Katz, "Issues in the Separation of Judaism and Christianity after 70 C.E.; A Reconsideration," *JBL* 103 (1984) 43–76, esp. 63–76.

9. Harrington, *Gospel of Matthew*, 10–22.

10. Davies, *Setting*, 290, fn 3; 332.

11. Bornkamm, "End-Expectation and Church in Matthew," in *Tradition and Interpretation in Matthew*, 39. For a similar position, see Kilpatrick, *Origin*, 122; Barth, "Matthew's Understanding of the Law," *Tradition and Interpretation in Matthew*, 58–164; Reinhart Hummel, *Die Auseinandersetzung zwischen Kirche und Judentum im Matthäusevangelium* (BEvTh 33; Munich: Kaiser, 1963) 32, 159–61; Betz, *Essays*, 21–22, 46, 62, 65. For critique, Stanton, *Gospel*, 118–24.

12. Stendahl, *School of St. Matthew*, xi–xiii; Schweizer, *Good News*, 16; Kümmel, *Introduction to the New Testament*, 114–15; Gundry, *Matthew*, 601; Guelich, *Sermon on the Mount*, 26; Kingsbury, *Matthew's Story of Jesus*, 154–56; Harrington, *Gospel of Matthew*, 8, 16.

13. Günther Bornkamm, "Die Binde- und Lösegewalt in der Kirche des Matthäus" in *Geschichte und Glaube II* (ed. Günther Bornkamm; BEvTh 53; Munich: Kaiser 1971) 37–50, esp. 40; in an English version, "The Authority to 'Bind' and 'Loose' in the Church in Matthew's Gospel: The Problem of Sources in Matthew's Gospel," in *Jesus and Man's Hope*, vol. I

(ed. Donald G. Miller; Perspective: Pittsburgh Theological Seminary, 1970) 37–50, esp. 41.

14. Douglas R. A. Hare, *The Theme of Jewish Persecution of Christians in the Gospel According to St. Matthew* (SNTSMS 6; Cambridge: Cambridge University, 1967) 80–145.

15. Graham Stanton, "The Gospel of Matthew and Judaism," *BJRL* 66 (1984) 264–84; idem, *Gospel*, 2–3, 85–107, 124–31, 322–23. A key aspect of Stanton's analysis in *Gospel for a New People* is that the Sermon shares the same *Sitz im Leben* as the gospel (322). He also suggests (*Gospel*, 169–91) that Christological factors influenced the separation.

16. Keith W. Clark, "The Gentile Bias in Matthew," *JBL* 66 (1947) 165–72; Poul Nepper-Christensen, *Das Matthäusevangelium— ein judenchristliches Evangelium?* (Acta Theologica Danica; Aarhus: Universitetsforlaget, 1958); Strecker, *Der Weg*, 15–35, 138–43; *Sermon on the Mount*, 43–44; Sjef van Tilborg, *The Jewish Leaders in Matthew* (Leiden: E. J. Brill, 1972) 171–72.

17. John P. Meier, *Law and History in Matthew's Gospel: A Redactional Study of Mt. 5:17–48* (Analecta Biblica 71; Rome: Biblical Institute, 1976); 7–24; idem, *The Vision of Matthew: Christ, Church and Morality in the First Gospel* (Theological Inquiries; New York: Paulist, 1979) 12–25.

18. For discussion see Stanton, *Gospel*, 131–39.

19. Waetjen, *Origin and Destiny*, 26–45.

20. H. D. Betz, "The Sermon on the Mount in Matthew's Interpretation," in *The Future of Early Christianity: Essays in Honor of Helmut Koester* (ed. B. A. Pearson; Minneapolis: Fortress, 1991) 258–75.

21. Barth, "Matthew's Understanding of the Law," *Tradition and Interpretation*, 75–76, 159–64. Others who adopt the view that there are antinomians in the community include Hummel, *Auseinandersetzung*, 64–66; Eduard Schweizer, "Observance

of the Law and Charismatic Activity in Matthew," *NTS* 16 (1969–70) 213–30, esp. 216–226; Schweizer, *Good News*, 178–82; Waetjen, *Origin and Destiny*, 110–11; Goulder, *Lection and Midrash*, 307–08; Jean Zumstein, *La Condition du croyant dans l'évangile selon Matthieu* (OBO 16; Göttingen: Vandenhoeck und Ruprecht, 1977) 171–200; Hendrickx, *Sermon on the Mount*, 162–71; Lambrecht, *Sermon*, 90.

22. Johannes Weiss, *The History of Primitive Christianity*, vol 2 (New York: Wilson-Erickson, 1947) 751–56, esp. 753; Streeter, *Four Gospels*, 256–57; Thomas W. Manson, *The Sayings of Jesus* (London: SCM, 1949) 24–25; Betz, *Essays*, 21–22, 49–51, 154–57; for discussion, Davies, *Setting*, 316–66, esp. 334–36; Stanton, *Gospel*, 311–14.

23. Strecker, *Der Weg*, 137, note 4; Strecker, *Sermon on the Mount*, 160–62; also Stendahl, *School of St. Matthew*, xii; Kümmel, *Introduction*, 117; Davies and Allison, *Matthew*, 501, n. 54; Stanton, *Gospel*, 47–49.

24. Harrington, *Gospel of Matthew*, 110.

25. So also Gundry, *Matthew*, 132–33.

26. Leland J. White, "Grid and Group in Matthew's Community: The Righteousness/Honor Code in the Sermon on the Mount," *Semeia* 35 (1986) 61–90.

27. See the redaction studies of Jack Dean Kingsbury, *The Parables of Jesus in Matthew 13* (Richmond: John Knox, 1969) 134–35; William G. Thompson, *Matthew's Advice to a Divided Community, Matthew 17:22–18:35* (Analecta Biblica 44; Rome: Biblical Press, 1970); for literary studies, Kingsbury, *Matthew as Story*, chapter 9; also Warren Carter, *Discipleship and Households: A Study of Matthew 19–20* (Sheffield: Sheffield Academic, forthcoming).

28. Eduard Schweizer, *Matthäus und seine Gemeinde* (SBS 71: Stuttgart: KBW, 1974).

29. Schweizer, *Good News*, 186, 189.

30. Jack Dean Kingsbury, "The Verb AKOLOUTHEIN ("To Follow") as an Index of Matthew's View of His Community," *JBL* 97 (1978) 56–73.

31. See Goulder, *Midrash*, 311, for a summary chart, and chapters 12–14 for discussion of the Sermon on the Mount.

32. Goulder, *Midrash*, chapter 9, esp. 172, 176–80. It should be noted that earlier somewhat similar proposals had been made (for Mark) by Philip Carrington, *The Primitive Christian Calendar* (Cambridge University Press, 1952) and (for Matthew) by Kilpatrick, *Origins of the Gospel*, chapters 4–5.

33. For discussion, see Goulder, *Midrash*, ch. 9, esp. 184–86; chs. 12–14.

34. See Leon Morris, "The Gospels and the Jewish Lectionaries," in *Gospel Perspectives* vol III (eds. Richard T. France and David Wenham; Sheffield: JSOT, 1983) 129–56, esp. 134–49.

4
The Content of the Sermon on the Mount: Part I

Joachim Jeremias formulated the central problem of the Sermon on the Mount as, "What is the meaning of the Sermon on the Mount?"[1] He summarized three answers which had been offered since 1900: 1) the Sermon teaches an ethical perfectionism, an obedience ethic for daily life, law not gospel;[2] 2) the Sermon provides an impossible ideal which condemns human beings, compelling readers to call out for God's mercy;[3] 3) the Sermon offers an interim ethic, a final urgent call to repentance in the short time before the end.[4] But when this eschatological crisis has passed, it does not offer a long-term "culture-ethic."

Jeremias finds each view inadequate. He proposes that the Sermon presumes the prior proclamation of the gospel which makes available to people the gift of God's grace. On this basis, the Sermon challenges people to make God's gift "the basis for [one's] life." The Sermon "delineates a lived faith" (34–35).

Jeremias' question, summary and alternative proposal

have been frequent starting points for scholars since 1960. In this chapter we will consider some discussions of individual sections of the Sermon. It will be clear that i) the various positions summarized by Jeremias continue to be advocated in relation to particular parts of the Sermon and that ii) new and different interpretations are being offered.

The Setting, Audience and Content of the Sermon

Discussion of the Sermon's meaning raises four preliminary issues. The first concerns the identity of the Sermon's speaker. By 5:1 Jesus has been identified by a significant array of titles: son of Abraham and son of David (1:1), Christ (1:17; 2:4), Emmanuel (1:23), God's Son (2:15; 3:17; 4:3, 6). He speaks as the one commissioned and favored by God.

A second issue concerns the significance of the "mountain" location for the Sermon (5:1). Luz is one of many commentators who sees in this location an attempt to associate Jesus and Moses (224). The phrase "he went up on the mountain" is used frequently in Exodus to denote Moses' ascent on Mount Sinai (Exod 19:3, 12; 24:15, 18; 34:2–4). The nature of the relationship between Jesus and Moses has, however, been debated. Luz rejects the view that Jesus' Sermon is antithetical to Moses' teaching, that Jesus is a second Moses who invalidates the first law. Rather for Luz, Jesus' Sermon on a mountain shows God to be again speaking in a fundamental way to Israel. The Sermon itself will demonstrate the relationship between Jesus' gospel and Moses' teaching,[5] a relationship which, for Luz, presumes fundamental continuity.

Others are not convinced that any association with Moses is suggested. Guelich argues that the Sermon "transcends the 'mosaic categories' of the Law, Sinai and Moses rather than offering the Christian counterpart of same." Hendrickx and Strecker see the mountain as a place of revelation,[6] while Waetjen views it as a place of enthronement for the church's Lord.[7] Terence Donaldson argues that "the mountain of teaching" is an eschatological site. He sees Zion rather than Sinai traditions informing the use of the mountain location in 5:1 and throughout Matthew's gospel. Israel's eschatological hopes and expectations centered on Zion are reinterpreted and fulfilled in Christological terms. "Jesus, and not Jerusalem, is the gathering point for the eschatological people of God and the locus of the renewal of Torah." The Sermon is the "authoritative declaration of the characteristics" of this community of Jews and Gentiles who are sent in mission to the world.[8] For these interpreters it is the identity of Jesus and his relationship to the promised new age (the eschatological setting and community) that are most significant for the Sermon's meaning.

The third issue concerns the Sermon's audience. Who is hearing or reading the Sermon? Answering this question is complicated by some ambiguity in the Sermon's introduction and conclusion. In 5:1, Jesus "sees the crowds," goes up the mountain, and, when his disciples come to him, teaches "them" (5:1). While it seems that Jesus' audience consists only of the disciples, the end of the Sermon notes the crowds' response of astonishment to Jesus' teaching (7:28–29). In Matthew's story, disciples as well as the crowds hear the Sermon. What, then, is the relationship between the crowd and the disciples? Are disciples distinguished from the crowds or part of the same group? Does the Sermon function in the same way for both groups? Gundry argues that there is no distinction between the disciples and crowds. Both groups receive Jesus' ministry in 4:17–25 and represent the true and false members of Matthew's community.[9]

Most commentators, however, see 5:1–2 distinguishing

the two groups. Most see the disciples as representatives of Matthew's community who have responded to Jesus' gift and call with obedient faith,[10] while the crowds represent Israel or those outside the church who may have encountered Jesus' gift (4:23–25) but who now must decide how to respond to his demand for a life of discipleship. The Sermon is thus primarily addressed to disciples to instruct them about an ethic of discipleship. These "disciples" are characters within the gospel narrative as well as the Christian readers of the Sermon. The wider circle of the crowd has been interpreted as signifying the Sermon's impact on society. Its content has been seen to function variously for this audience as a proclamation by the people of God of "God's will for the whole world" (Luz), as presenting God's "demand" (Davies and Allison, Strecker, Schweizer) or God's invitation to Israel and all people (Hamm, Hendrickx, Donaldson), as challenging Israel to find in Jesus' teaching the authentic interpretation of God's will (Harrington), as dividing disciples (those who "hear and do," 7:24) from those who are "astonished" (Guelich).[11]

Fourth, discussions of the Sermon's content have understood the "meaning" of the Sermon to embrace two interrelated dimensions. In 5:17 readers are warned about *thinking* or *understanding* in a particular way. Yet several verses later in 5:21–48, what disciples *do* in their daily lives is the particular concern. Though the Sermon clearly regards these two dimensions as integrally connected (see 7:24–27), we will somewhat arbitrarily divide this material. In this chapter we will focus more on the discussions about *understanding* parts of the Sermon, while in the next chapter we will focus on the discussions about *living* the Sermon. We will need, though, to remind ourselves continually of the unity of the material in presenting a coherent vision of discipleship. The "meaning" of the Sermon embraces both aspects: "genuine faith in Christ must be demonstrated in daily obedience to the way of life he proclaimed."[12]

The Beatitudes: 5:3–12

The title of Robert Guelich's article "The Matthean Beatitudes: 'Entrance-Requirements' or Eschatological Blessings?" expresses two ways in which scholars have interpreted the role of the beatitudes at the start of the Sermon.[13] Strecker argues that the beatitudes present "entrance requirements" or ethical demands which people must realize in their lives if they are to be admitted to the yet future kingdom of heaven.[14] The first beatitude requires humility, the second grief over sin, the third and fourth require deeds determined by goodness. The beatitudes are imperatives that "summon the hearers to something they do not possess as yet, but through their actions are supposed to realize" (33). The first part of each beatitude provides norms and demands for the lives of Jesus' followers while the second part pledges entry into the future kingdom for those who live this way.

Important for Strecker's analysis is his claim that Matthew's redaction has ethicized and spiritualized the beatitudes which he received from the tradition (see chapter 1 above). For instance, the fourth beatitude (5:6) reframes Q's blessing on those who are literally hungry to pronounce a blessing on those who hunger for righteousness. Matthew's redacted form now requires from followers "a decisive ethical initiative" through active deeds (37).

Guelich is not convinced by this analysis.[15] As we noted in chapter 1, Guelich argues that Matthew's redaction is guided not by a desire to ethicize the beatitudes but by a desire to bring them into line with Isaiah 61. This goal is intended to demonstrate that God was at work in Jesus Messiah accomplishing his redemptive purposes for humankind. The initiative in this fulfillment process of Jesus' ministry is clearly divine, and the Beatitudes must be understood from that perspective or the human component is completely distorted in terms of the doctrine of merit and reward. (110)

For Guelich, the beatitudes address those who have already encountered God's saving initiative, call and demand in Jesus and have responded positively to it. The attitudes and conduct required in the beatitudes are commensurate with and reflective of this experience. The beatitudes declare the blessing of the new eschatological reality that has entered the human realm in Jesus. Disciples are given the assuring promises of participation in the future consummation of God's reign in the knowledge that God's redemptive presence has already impacted their lives.

Several significant differences are evident in these two readings. While Strecker stresses human response, Guelich's emphasis falls on God's initiative. While Strecker stresses human performance and demand, Guelich emphasizes God's gracious gift. While Strecker looks to the future for the presence of the kingdom, Guelich sees it already shaping the present.

These differences are evident in their two quite different interpretations of the term "righteousness" (5:6, 10). Strecker interprets the term as indicating ethical conduct which is consistent with God's will. Such ethical conduct is required if one is to enter the kingdom in the future.[16] Guelich does not deny that the term has an ethical component but he sees the ethical dimension resulting from the term's *primary* reference to God's saving action. The term "righteousness" expresses "both the eschatological gift of the new relationship between God and the individual as well as the resultant 'ethical conduct' towards God (6:1–18) and others (5:21–48) made possible through the 'gift.' "[17]

A clue from the context in which the Sermon appears in Matthew's gospel may lend support to Guelich's analysis. The beatitudes follow the beginning of Jesus' ministry in 4:17 in which Jesus announces the presence of the kingdom of heaven. In the following verses (4:18–25), several scenes indicate what happens when God's reign is among human beings in Jesus. People respond to God's gift and claim on their lives by committing themselves to him (4:18–22) while others experience wholeness (4:23–25). The sequence of the narrative with the repetition of the word "kingdom" from 4:17 in 4:23 and in the first and eighth beatitudes (5:3, 10) suggests that the beatitudes are addressed to those who have already encountered the presence and gift of God's reign.

Further, it should also be remembered that those who make up the audience of Matthew's gospel are, as we observed in the last chapter, already *disciples* of Jesus. The beatitudes shape an identity and lifestyle commensurate with their experience of God's saving presence among them.

5:17–20

These frequently-discussed verses form a very important section of the Sermon. In defining the relationship between Jesus and the Jewish scriptures ("the law and the prophets"), they address an issue that is regarded by many scholars as having been of central importance for Matthew's community in its separation from the synagogue and for its self-definition. Redaction critics carefully sift through these verses to identify traditional and redactional material, thereby gaining some insight into the contours and history of this debate.[18]

Further, most scholars see these verses as introducing the content of the Sermon's central section since the phrase "law and the prophets" is repeated in 7:12. This repetition ensures that 5:17 and 7:12 form a framework around the central section. 5:20 demands from Matthew's community a "righteousness" which "exceeds that of the scribes and Pharisees." Most scholars think that 5:21–48 provides six examples of this "righteousness." The repetition of the word "righteousness" in 6:1 (often translated as "piety") indicates that chapter 6 continues the instruction about what constitutes this way of life.[19]

Hans Dieter Betz suggests that 5:17–20 contributes in another way. He argues that it presents the four "hermeneutical principles which guided Jesus in his interpretation of the Torah."[20] The four guiding principles define "the text, the teacher, the teaching and the recipients of the teaching" (39). The first principle (5:17) with its affirmation that Jesus "fulfills the law and the prophets" declares Jesus' life-mission and teaching as found in the Sermon to be orthodox within Judaism. The second principle (5:18) recognizes that "the scriptural authority of [the Hebrew text of] the Torah will not pass away so long as the conditions of this transitory world persist" (45). The third principle (5:19) "seeks to establish the binding force of Jesus' interpretation of the Torah for teachers in the community" addressed by the Sermon (50). The fourth principle (5:20) defines the goal of Jesus' teaching. The Sermon does not provide legal requirements but educates disciples to recognize the demands of God and to do justice in their thought and conduct to the will of God. This is the righteousness which contrasts with and exceeds that of "the scribes and the Pharisees," and which is recognized "by the divine judge in the last judgment" (53).

But while many would agree that 5:17–20 provides important clues for interpreting 5:21–7:12, the content of these four verses continues to be debated by scholars. For example, the verb "fulfill" in verse 17 (πληρόω) has been widely discussed.[21] Scholars have tried different methods to define its meaning: some have looked at possible equivalent Hebrew and Aramaic terms; others have paid particular attention to the word's use in non-biblical or Septuagint Greek; others have looked to the context of Matthew's gospel. Most have also noticed that the meaning one attributes to 5:17 is also significantly impacted by one's understanding of the time-frame indicated by the two "until" (temporal) clauses in 5:18.

For example, Patte sees the struggle of Jesus and Satan over the correct interpretation of scripture (4:1–11) as providing the clue to understanding "fulfill" as "allowing the law to mold one's will, to define one's vocation . . . which determines the way one acts." 5:21–48 "describe[s] what should be the disciples' implementation of their vocation established with the help of scripture."[22]

Other scholars have understood Matthew's declaration that Jesus *fulfills* the law as a reference to Jesus doing or actualizing the requirements of the law, the will of God, in his teaching and life.[23] This establishing or accomplishing of the law is understood in terms of love (7:12; 22:36–40),[24] and by others as Jesus bringing out the inner or original demands of the law.[25] Jesus' teaching therefore establishes the validity of the law until the end of the age.

Another line of interpretation rejects the view that 5:17 means "to do, obey, or put into practice" the law. John P. Meier argues that other verbs express the sense of "doing" or "keeping" commandments.[26] He notices that Matthew uses the verb translated "fulfill" predominantly to introduce quotations from the Hebrew Bible.[27] The verb expresses the sense of Jesus bringing into being what is promised in the Hebrew scriptures, "the law and the prophets" (76–82). The comprehensive nature of this phrase as a reference to the Hebrew scriptures indicates that the "doing" of the law is too narrow a focus for any interpretation.

For Meier, the phrase invokes the larger context of salvation history (the larger story of God's saving actions toward human beings). Both the law and the prophetic writings point ahead to the new age now being brought into being by Jesus. Meier finds support for his interpretation of the prophetic function of the law in 11:13. In that verse "law" along with "prophets" form the subject of the verb "prophesied" (85–89). Thus for Meier the law and the prophets functioned in salvation history for a particular period of time with their prophetic role. They pointed ahead to Jesus; with the coming of Jesus, the predicted new age has dawned and the law and the prophets now cease to function in that way.[28]

Meier finds further support for his analysis in 5:18. Matthew's Jesus declares that "till heaven and earth pass away, not an iota, not a dot, will pass from the law until all is accomplished." Scholars have interpreted the time framework in this verse in at least three ways. i) Some understand 5:18 as declaring that the law in even the smallest detail will remain valid forever. This view understands the two temporal clauses ("until heaven and earth pass away"; "until all is accomplished") as indicating "never."[29] ii) Others see a reference to the law's continuing validity until the yet-future end of this age. We noted above that Betz is close to this latter position when he interprets 5:18 to indicate that "the scriptural authority of the Torah will not pass away so long as the conditions of this transitory world persist."[30]

Meier does not accept these interpretations. He argues that the phrase "until heaven and earth pass away" reflects Jewish apocalyptic expectations that this age and world will end when God creates the new world. The law functions prophetically until that time. The second "until" clause ("until all is accomplished") further defines the time period in which the law functions prophetically by indicating when the new world and age come about. The verb translated as "accomplished" (or "come to pass") is not used elsewhere by Matthew to indicate "doing" or "observing" the commands of the law. Rather it appears in several introductions to the citations from the Hebrew Bible which indicate that Jesus is bringing into being what the "law and the prophets" prophesied (1:22; 21:4; 26:54–56). This use indicates for Meier that in verse 18 Matthew understands the new age to have already dawned in the life, death and resurrection of Jesus.[31] With the passing away of the old age in the coming of Jesus, the prophetic function of the law and the prophets has ceased. Jesus' teaching and actions, which include his interpretation of the law (5:21–48), now provide the center and norms for Christian existence (5:19–20; 89–124).[32]

The Six "Antitheses" of 5:21–48

Most commentators understand the antitheses as providing examples of the "greater righteousness" demanded of disciples (5:20). Two issues dominate the contemporary discussion of this section: i) With whom is Jesus arguing—contemporary interpreters of the law or with Moses as recorded in the Hebrew Bible? ii) Does Jesus' teaching stand in continuity or discontinuity with the Hebrew Bible and/or Jewish traditions? Or to express it another way, what is the relationship between the two parts of the six statements, the first part introduced by "you have heard it said . . ." and the second by "But I say to you . . ."? Does Matthew's Jesus "fulfill" the law by staying within its requirements or by transcending or revoking it with new teaching?

The Jewish scholar Pinchas Lapide argues that it is a mistake to call the six sections of 5:21–48 "antitheses."[33] In none of the six sayings is Jesus' teaching antithetical or a "counter claim that would contradict a previously stated thesis." The phrase that introduces Jesus' teaching "But I say to you" employs a construction from "rabbinic rhetoric" which functions to elucidate a previous statement (44). The construction places Jesus' teaching clearly within the debates and dialogues of "pluralistic Judaism" (45). It distinguishes his teaching from that of others and expresses teachings which "deepen, intensify and radicalize the biblical commandments—guiding us back to their roots and original intentions" (46). Lapide's discussion of the six "supertheses" establishes significant points of similarity and difference between Jesus and rabbinic interpreters (49–135).

Though not sharing Lapide's emphasis on the context of debate within contemporary Judaism, Luz also underlines continuity between Jesus' teaching and the tradition. He sees all six antitheses as a "radical intensification of individual Old Testament commands" (270).[34] It is the demand of love that provides the center for this intensification (270, 279). The first antithesis (5:21–26) intensifies the command against killing by identifying God's demand on the whole person for a comprehensive love which includes even enemies (285–90). The second antithesis against adultery (5:27–30) intensifies the commandment against adultery with a concern for "the integrity of the woman and/or the sanctity of God-ordained marriage" (296). The fifth antithesis (5:38–42) intensifies the Old Testament's concern to limit revenge. Love is the renunciation of counterforce and resistance (331), just as in the last antithesis (5:43–48) it is to be extended even to enemies (342–43).

Luz concedes some difficulty with his claim that all six

"antitheses" are intensifications of Hebrew Bible commands. The fourth and fifth antitheses (concerning oaths and retaliation, 5:33–42) particularly pose problems.[35] With regard to verse 33 Luz notes that "the Old Testament law of God has been surpassed by Jesus' proclamation. This surpassing involves not only an element of deepening . . . but also an element of abrogation, namely the rejection of the oath" (317). And in discussing the relation between Jesus' prohibition on revenge and the Old Testament in 5:38, Luz notes that "Matthew introduces redactionally an Old Testament principle which can only be understood as a contrast to the words of Jesus." This formulation is "less that of fulfillment than of an antithesis to the Old Testament" (330).

Such difficulties are central for Meier's discussion of 5:21–48.[36] He argues (as does Luz, 270–72) that the interpretation of 5:21–48 must be consistent with one's interpretation of 5:17–20. If it can be shown that in 5:21–48 "some antitheses do revoke the letter of the Law . . . then the view that Mt simply portrays Jesus as the one who confirms, explains, fulfills and radicalizes the Law is inadequate" (125). Having argued that the prophetic function of the law and the prophets has ended, and that now Jesus' teaching and interpretation of the law guide the Christian community, Meier is open to the possibility that Matthew's Jesus will in places revoke aspects of the law.

Meier argues that in fact three "antitheses revoke the letter of the Law" while three "radicalize and internalize the Law without revoking it."[37] In the latter category belong the first two and the last antitheses (5:21–26, 27–30, 43–48). In each of these antitheses, Meier understands that the initial phrase "You have heard that it was said" (5:21a, 26a, 43a) names requirements given by God to the Israelites at Sinai and recorded in the written Torah (131–34). Jesus' teaching is introduced by the authoritative "But I say to you" (5:22, 28, 44). In these three instances, Meier agrees with Lapide and Luz in claiming that Jesus "sharpens, radicalizes, internalizes the Torah, going beyond the letter to the ultimate intention of the Torah" (134–35). In the first and second, Jesus identifies anger as being as serious as murder and a lustful heart and glances as bad as adultery. The sixth extends love for neighbor to include the enemy (136–38).

In the remaining three antitheses (5:31–32, 33–37, 38–42), the first part also names God's requirements recorded in the Torah, while the second part offers Jesus' teaching. However, Meier argues that in these three antitheses the relationship between the two parts is quite different. "The word of Jesus stands . . . in contrast to the Word of God as expressed in the Torah; and, when this takes place, the word of Jesus is to be the decisive norm for the disciples' life" (134). In 5:31–32, the law's permission to divorce is overturned, except for the situation of Gentile converts who find that their marriage is incestuous as defined in Leviticus 18:6–18 (140–50).[38] In 5:33–37, the taking of oaths and vows, permitted in the Mosaic law (for example Exod 22:6–7, 10; Deut 6:13; 10:20), is now forbidden (150–56). In 5:38–42, the law of revenge (Exod 21:24; Lev 24:20; Deut 19:21) is revoked (159–61).

Meier sees in these six antitheses Jesus teaching the "greater justice" demanded in 5:20. These antitheses are part of Jesus' teaching which portrays the "radicalized internalized Christian justice which can abrogate the letter of the Torah." This "radicalized will of God" which belongs to the new age present in the risen Jesus is to be observed in the Christian community (160–61).[39]

Davies and Allison take a somewhat different approach. Against Meier's position but in agreement with

Lapide, they argue that 5:21–48 are not antitheses because "Jesus does not overturn the Pentateuch." Jesus' words are not an interpretation or contradiction of the Torah, nor (against Lapide, Harrington) do they polemicize against Jewish interpretations of scripture. The concept of "interpretation" inadequately describes the relationship between the two parts of each saying. Since the authority for Jesus' declarations is located in his own person (*"I* say to you"), the Torah does nothing more than supply the point of departure for Jesus' teaching. In each instance *Jesus demands more than the Torah but without contradicting it.* The structure of the sayings points to this "more" that Jesus requires. The Greek word which introduces Jesus' statements and is usually translated as "but" (δέ) does not signal a strong contrast. Rather it has a "continuative function" which expresses the sense of "in addition." Jesus' teaching does not contradict the Torah or dispute other interpretations; it moves beyond what is present in the Old Testament.[40]

The six scenes provide concrete examples of the attitude and behaviors Jesus requires. Disciples are to strive for purity of intention (5:21–30), for obedience to God's will (5:31–37), for unselfish love for friend and enemy (5:38–42). The scenes show how Jesus' demands surpass those of the Torah without contradicting it. The "greater righteousness" (5:20) is not constituted by legal norms, though they are helpful. Rather, it derives from the unquantifiable things such as love of God and neighbor, from those who are genuinely poor in spirit, pure in heart, full of mercy. It means not only the absence of murder, but also of hate, not only the absence of adulterous behavior but the absence of lust. 5:21–48 exemplifies this "more," this quest "which was not, in Matthew's eyes, equally enjoined by Moses."[41]

Davies and Allison's claim that in each of the six scenes Jesus demands more than the Torah but without contradicting it can be tested in relation to the three scenes that caused some difficulty for Luz and which provided the basis for Meier's claim that Jesus does revoke the law. Davies and Allison's discussion of 5:31–32 and 5:33–37 acknowledges some contradiction,[42] while in 5:38–42 they argue there is no contradiction. In that scene Jesus' teaching does not address the Hebrew Bible's institutionalizing of revenge but addresses only its absence from personal relationships (542).

The Lord's Prayer (6:9–13)

We have already noted that several scholars see the Lord's Prayer as being central to the Sermon. What do disciples pray for in the Lord's Prayer? Raymond Brown outlines a view that has been widely supported. For members of Matthew's community, "the prayer given by Jesus was an expression of their yearning for His return and for the ultimate fulfillment of the things He had promised."[43] Brown sees the prayer as an eschatological prayer in which the petitions "do not refer to daily circumstances but to the final times" involving the return of Christ and the destruction of the forces of evil (217–18). The first three petitions pray for different aspects of the same reality, that God would at the final time bring about the completion of God's saving plan for heaven and earth (237–38). To pray for our "future bread" is to pray for one's participation in the heavenly banquet (243). To pray for forgiveness and deliverance is to request the "final pardon of debts" at the judgment (247) when God is victorious over the evil one, Satan (248–53). On this reading, the prayer focuses on the future and on what God will do.

Other scholars, though, see an emphasis on the present and on the actions of those who pray the prayer rather than on God's future actions. For example, Luz concludes that only the second petition ("Your kingdom come") has an undoubted "eschatological element" (377–78). To pray "Your will be done" is not to pray for God to establish God's saving will at the end time, but on the basis of i) parallels in Jewish prayers, ii) the emphasis in the wording on "earth" as the place for doing God's will, and iii) parallels with the rest of the gospel (cf. 26:42), this petition seeks the "strength to subordinate oneself actively to the will of God." It "aims at the active behavior of the person" (380). The fourth petition seeks not participation in the final banquet but that God will provide the minimum nourishment necessary for survival (382–83). The final petition does not seek deliverance from the final struggle with Satan but for God's power in the midst of everyday temptations and experiences of evil (384–85).

It is very significant for Luz that the prayer is placed at the center of the Sermon and following the instruction about lifestyle in chapter 5. After confronting disciples "with the demand for higher righteousness and perfection," Matthew leads them "into the inner space of prayer . . . through action to grace." The way is "from the practice of perfection into prayer to the Father and then back again to the fruits of good works." The doing or acting of disciples "remains constantly dependent on prayer" (388–89).

Guelich also seeks a greater balance between the future and present elements, between God's actions and those of disciples.[44] He recognizes in the first three petitions a concern for the final establishment of God's saving will and rule, but this expectation is based on the "present reality of God's reign in their lives," on the commitment to doing God's will in the present (310–11). With the fourth to seventh petitions (6:11–13, "Give us this day . . .") the orientation to the present and the life of the one who prays is foremost. These petitions request that "the ultimate blessings for the day of salvation become a part of one's *present* experience" (315). In this way, present and future are vitally connected.

Two Difficult Verses (5:48; 7:6)

The command in 5:48 to be "perfect" has long troubled interpreters. Scholars have sought to make sense of this verse in relation to the rest of chapter 5 and in terms of how the word "perfect" is used in the Septuagint, the Greek translation of the Hebrew Bible. Since 5:21, Matthew's Jesus has been teaching the will of God. 5:48 is generally understood to be a summary of Jesus' demand that disciples live the will of God as he has interpreted it. In the Septuagint, to be "perfect" means to be whole-hearted, to be complete or whole. Hence the "perfection" demanded by the Sermon is a wholehearted focus on God's will. To live this way is the imitation of God (5:48b). Guelich emphasizes that such living results from a new relationship with God created by God's gift (cf. 5:45).[45]

The command in 7:6 not to give dogs what is holy or to throw one's pearls before swine has also been difficult to interpret. Part of the problem is how to relate the verse to what precedes it; a further difficulty is to know what "dogs, pearls and swine" indicate. One reading has suggested that, since sacrificial offerings are referred to as "holy" in Exodus (29:33; Lev 2:3), the readers are reminded not to let unclean things (dogs and swine) corrupt them. But the appropriateness of this reading is dubious since the temple was destroyed in 70 CE by the Romans. A second possibility sees "dogs" as a reference to Gentiles (15:26–27) and interprets the verse as forbidding preaching the precious gospel ("pearls") to Gentiles. But this reading is also unlikely since Matthew's gospel commands such preaching (28:18–20). We noted a third read-

ing in chapter 2, Bornkamm's suggestion (supported by
Guelich) that the verse should be linked with the petition in
the Lord's prayer for faithfulness in the face of temptation
and evil (6:13). A fourth reading (Waetjen) interprets the
verses as referring to people described in 6:19–7:5 who have
no concern for the human wholeness outlined in that section
and who respond with violent anger to such talk.[46] Davies and
Allison take seriously the connection with 7:1–5, understanding 7:6 to counter an extreme interpretation of those verses.
While 7:1–5 indicates that there must not be too much sever-
ity in community relationships, 7:6 establishes that there must
not be too much laxity.[47]

Conclusion

From our discussion of these important sections several
issues have emerged which are central for determining the
meaning of the Sermon. One of these issues concerns the
relationship of the present and the future. While most commentators recognize in the Sermon an orientation to the
future coming of God's reign, it is evident in the discussions
of the beatitudes and the Lord's Prayer that many scholars
see the future as already impacting the present.

A second issue concerns the relationship between Jesus'
teaching and that of Jewish tradition. We have seen diverse
opinions about the meaning of the word "fulfill" (5:17) and
about how to relate the two parts of the initial statements of
the so-called "antitheses" in 5:21–48. Most scholars struggle
with assessing continuities and discontinuities between Matthew's Jesus and the Jewish tradition.

One issue, though, on which there does seem to be
universal agreement is that the meaning of the Sermon is not
restricted to "right thinking." The Sermon requires a way of

life from its hearers. That way of life is the focus of the next chapter.

Notes

1. Joachim Jeremias, *The Sermon on the Mount* (FBBS; Philadelphia: Fortress, 1959, 1963) 1.

2. For example, Hans Windisch, *The Meaning of the Sermon on the Mount* (Philadelphia: Westminster, 1951).

3. Jeremias (*Sermon*, 6) called this the view of Lutheran orthodoxy.

4. Albert Schweitzer, *The Mystery of the Kingdom of God* (New York: Dodd and Mead, 1914) 97.

5. Hare, *Matthew*, 34–35; Stanton, *Gospel*, 80; Harrington, *Matthew*, 82; Davies and Allison, *Matthew*, 422–25; Patte, *Matthew*, 61–62; Pinchas Lapide, *The Sermon on the Mount* (Maryknoll: Orbis, 1986) 11–12; Gundry, *Matthew*, 66; Benjamin Bacon, *Studies in Matthew*, (New York: Holt, 1930) 81–82, 339.

6. Davies, *Setting of the Sermon on the Mount*, 14–108; Guelich, *Sermon on the Mount*, 55; Strecker, *Sermon*, 24–25; Lambrecht, *Sermon*, 9; Meier, *Vision of Matthew*, 49–51, 62–66, 222–23.

7. Waetjen, *Origin and Destiny*, 84–85.

8. Terence Donaldson, *Jesus on the Mountain: A Study in Matthean Theology* (JSNTSS 8; Sheffield: University of Sheffield, 1985) 105–21, esp. 115, 118, 203–13. For critique, Dale Allison, "Jesus and Moses (Mt 5:1–2)," *ExposT* 98 (1987) 203–05.

9. Gundry, *Matthew*, 65–66, 137; Patte (*Matthew*, 62) sees the "crowds as disciples or possibly as potential disciples."

10. Ulrich Luz, "The Disciples in the Gospel according to Matthew," in *The Interpretation of Matthew* (ed. Graham Stanton; London, Philadelphia: SPCK and Fortress, 1983) 98–128.

11. Harrington, *Gospel of Matthew*, 82; Dennis Hamm, *The Beatitudes in Context* (Wilmington: Michael Glazier, 1990) 77–78; Luz, *Matthew 1–7*, 216, 224; Davies and Allison, *Matthew 1–7*, 425–27, 725; Strecker, *Sermon*, 25–26; Donaldson, *Jesus on the Mountain*, 114–15; Hendrickx, *Sermon*, 8–9; Guelich, *Sermon on the Mount*, 51, 59; Schweizer, *Good News*, 78–79. For the role of the crowds in the gospel, Warren Carter, "The Crowds in Matthew's Gospel," *CBQ* 55 (1993) 54–67.

12. Hare, *Matthew*, 2.

13. Guelich's article appeared in *JBL* 95 (1976) 415–34; also *Sermon on the Mount*, 109–11.

14. Georg Strecker, "Die Makarismen der Bergpredigt," *NTS* 17 (1970–71) 255–75, esp. 259–63; idem, *Sermon*, 30–34; Luz, *Matthew 1–7*, 217. Earlier Windisch (*Meaning of the Sermon*, 26–27, 37–38, 87–88 note 31) had proposed this analysis.

15. Guelich, *Sermon*, 66, 109–11; Hare, *Matthew*, 35–38; Harrington, *Gospel of Matthew*, 82–83; Davies and Allison, *Matthew 1–7*, 439–40, 466.

16. Strecker, *Sermon on the Mount*, 37–38. Others support a focus on human action (though modifying aspects of Strecker's position): Luz, *Matthew 1–7*, 237–38; Davies and Allison, *Matthew 1–7*, 452–53; Benno Pryzybylski, *Righteousness in Matthew and His World of Thought* (SNTSMS 41; Cambridge: Cambridge University, 1980) 78–99.

17. Guelich, "Matthean Beatitudes," 426–31; idem, *Sermon*, 84–87; also Hendrickx, *Sermon*, 26; Hamm, *Beatitudes*, 95; Harrington, *Gospel of Matthew*, 79. Both Meier (*Tradition and History*, 76–79) and John Reumann (*Righteousness in the New Testament* [Philadelphia: Fortress, 1982] 125–35) find references to both divine salvific activity and human responsive action.

18. In addition to the commentaries, Robert J. Banks, "Matthew's Understanding of the Law; Authenticity and Reinterpretation in Matthew 5:17–20," *JBL* 93 (1974) 226–42; Robert G. Hamerton-Kelly, "Attitudes to the Law in Matthew's Gospel: a Discussion of Matthew 5:18," *Biblical Research* 17 (1972) 19–32.

19. For example, Barth, "Matthew's Understanding," 64–73; Meier, *Tradition and History*, 41–44.

20. Betz, "The Hermeneutical Principles of the Sermon on the Mount (Matt. 5:17–20)," in *Essays on the Sermon on the Mount*, 37–53.

21. Davies and Allison (*Matthew 1–7*, 485–86) list nine interpretations.

22. Patte, *Matthew*, 71–73, 77.

23. Barth, "Matthew's Understanding," 69; Hill, *Matthew*, 117; Strecker, *Sermon*, 53–56; Luz, *Matthew 1–7*, 264–72; Harrington, *Gospel of Matthew*, 83–84.

24. Barth, "Matthew's Interpretation," 64–73; Schweizer, *Good News*, 106–09; Hendrickx, *Sermon*, 47 (in part); Lapide, *Sermon on the Mount*, 14–15; Roger Mohrlang, *Matthew and Paul* (Cambridge: Cambridge University, 1984) 8–19, 25, 94–100; Lambrecht, *Sermon*, 87; Luz, *Matthew 1–7*, 268–71, 279; Klyne R. Snodgrass, "Matthew's Understanding of the Law," *Interpretation* 46 (1992) 368–78, esp. 369–75.

25. Alan McNeile, *The Gospel According to Matthew* (London: Macmillan, 1938) 58; Lambrecht, *Sermon*, 82–84; Waetjen, *Origin and Destiny*, 92; Albright and Mann, *Matthew*, 58; Hare, *Matthew*, 47.

26. Meier (*Law and History*, 70–72, 75) considers ποιεῖν ("do"; 5:19; 7:12, 21, 24; 8:9; 12:50; 19:16; 21:6, 31; 23:3, 23; 26:19), τηρεῖν ("keep"; 19:17; 23:3; 28:20), and φυλάσσω ("observe"; 19:20).

27. The verb πληρόω ("fulfill") appears sixteen times in Matthew. Meier (*Law and History*, 76) identifies twelve usages in which it introduces a Hebrew Bible citation (1:22; 2:15, 17, 23; 4:14; 8:17; 12:17; 13:35; 21:4; 26:54, 56; 27:9). The three remaining usages (3:15; 13:48; 23:32; [5:17 is the fourth]) "carry at least some nuance of eschatological consummation, prophetic fulfillment, or fulfillment of a preordained destiny" (80). For a summary, Meier, *Vision of Matthew*, 224–28.

28. Meier, *Tradition and History*, 82–89; also Banks, "Matthew's Understanding," 233, 242; Lapide, *Sermon*, 18–19 (the redactor's interpretation); Gundry, *Matthew*, 80–81; Davies and Allison, *Matthew 1–7*, 485–87.

29. Hill, *Gospel of Matthew*, 118; Strecker, *Sermon*, 55–56.

30. Betz, "Hermeneutical Principles," 45–46; Patte, *Gospel of Matthew*, 71–73; Davies and Allison (*Matthew 1–7*, 493–95) see the law remaining valid for Jewish Christians but Gentiles were not required to observe it.

31. Also Schweizer, *Good News*, 107–08; with some sympathy and hesitation, Stanton, *Gospel*, 300.

32. Meier, *Tradition and History*, 45–65; idem, *Vision of Matthew*, 229–34. Also Gundry, *Matthew*, 78–81; Guelich (*Sermon*, 138–49) distinguishes between meanings in the pre-Matthean tradition and in the Matthean understanding; Hendrickx, *Sermon*, 44–51; Banks, "Matthew's Understanding," 233–38; Kingsbury, *Matthew as Story*, 64–66; Davies and Allison, *Matthew 1–7*, 485–87.

33. Lapide, *Sermon on the Mount*, 45–46.

34. Also stressing a radicalizing or intensifying of the law's demands, and the continuity of Jesus' teaching with the Old Testament, Harrington, *Gospel of Matthew*, 86–92; Lambrecht, *Sermon*, 100–01; Hill, *Gospel of Matthew*, 119–20. Hare (*Matthew*, 50–62) sees love as the key element of this intensification.

35. It should also be noted that Luz (*Matthew 1–7*, 301–02) concedes some problems (though not as serious) with 5:31–32. Barth ("Matthew's Understanding," 92–95) essentially agrees with Luz's emphasis on the radicalizing of the law, but Barth concedes that in 5:38 "the Old Testament direction is completely overthrown" (94) and he is ambivalent about 5:31.

36. Meier, *Law and History*, Chapter 4, "The Antitheses— Confirmation of a Thesis"; idem, *Vision of Matthew*, 240–62.

37. Meier, *Law and History*, 136. Also Strecker, *Sermon on the Mount*, 94–95; Schweizer (*Good News*, 110–11) sees the first two antitheses strengthening two of the ten commandments, while the remaining four abrogate or abolish OT regulations. Lambrecht (*Sermon*, 101) and Waetjen (*Origin and Destiny*, 95–104) take a similar position.

38. For discussion of the exceptive clause, see chapter 5.

39. Guelich (*Sermon on the Mount*, 175–271) agrees with Meier's emphasis on the innovative nature and Christocentric basis of the antitheses (237–39, 255–62). However, he sees the fourth antithesis (5:33–37) belonging with the first two (5:21–26, 27–30) in "transcending or surpassing the premise rather than opposing it." The sixth (5:43–48) belongs with the third (5:31–32) and fifth (5:38–42) in "setting aside their corresponding premises" (177).

40. For a somewhat similar position, Snodgrass, "Matthew's Understanding," 374; Hendrickx, *Sermon on the Mount*, 60–96, esp. 61, 69; Gundry, *Matthew*, 82–84.

41. Davies and Allison, *Matthew 1–7*, 501–09; Stanton, *Gospel*, 301–03.

42. On 5:31–32, "the impression one gains from ancient Jewish sources is that divorce was relatively easy and was not considered a grave misdeed" (Davies and Allison, *Matthew 1–7*, 527–28); on 5:33–37, "The OT permits oaths in everyday

speech. . . . But with the followers of Jesus there should be no need for such oaths" (532–33).

43. Raymond Brown, "The Pater Noster as an Eschatological Prayer," *New Testament Essays* (New York: Paulist, 1965, 1982) 217–53, esp. 224; Albright and Mann, *Matthew*, 75–77; Hill, *Matthew*, 136–39 (generally); Davies and Allison, *Matthew*, 593–94; Harrington, *Gospel of Matthew*, 95–99.

44. For similar readings, Joachim Jeremias, *The Lord's Prayer* (FBBS: Philadelphia: Fortress, 1964) 16–33; Schweizer, *Good News*, 146–59; Hendrickx, *Sermon*, 108–24; Gundry, *Matthew*, 106–09; Strecker, *Sermon*, 105–28, esp. 112–16, 119–20, 122; Lambrecht, *Sermon*, 138–45; Patte, *Matthew*, 102–05; Hare, *Matthew*, 66–71.

45. Luz, *Matthew 1–7*, 346; Davies and Allison, *Matthew 1–7*, 561–63; Guelich, *Sermon*, 233–37. Rudolf Schnackenburg, "Christian Perfection According to Matthew," in *Christian Existence in the New Testament Vol 1* (Notre Dame: University of Notre Dame, 1968) 158–79.

46. Waetjen, *Origin and Destiny*, 108–09.

47. See the discussions in Luz, *Matthew 1–7*, 418–20; Davies and Allison, *Matthew 1–7*, 674–77; Guelich, *Sermon*, 353–56, 376–77.

5
The Content of the
Sermon on the Mount:
Part II

Most contemporary discussions of Matthew's Sermon affirm its concern with daily living. In the Sermon, understanding and practice are "indissolubly connected,"[1] as 5:17–20 and 7:24–27, for instance, explicitly underline. While the impracticability of the Sermon is regularly considered,[2] most recent discussion has centered on a cluster of three issues concerning the carrying out of its teaching: 1) What does the Sermon require? 2) And of whom? Given its address to a specific community of Christian disciples (chapter 3) what, if anything, does it say to contemporary disciples and/or to non-Christian society? And how do we determine that address? 3) What is the nature of Christian existence that it presents? What is the relationship between the Sermon's demands for human action and God's grace? What is the relationship between ethics and eschatology, its demands for disciples to live a particular way of life in the present and entrance to the reign of God at the end time?

The Nature of Christian Existence: Ethics and Eschatology

In addressing questions concerning the nature of Christian existence, Luz argues that grace and demand are intertwined in the Sermon. Grace does not precede the Sermon's demands but "grace happens in the proclamation of the demands" (215). This grace enables obedience. "Christ opens the way into life for those who *do* righteousness. . . . He gives his grace to the doers of the word." The experience of grace is found only in the practice of Jesus' commands, not in the hearing nor in the intention (454).

Further for Luz, "the practice of the disciples is . . . not an 'ethical' sign of the new world already dawning" (217). Rather it is "the expression of the will of God as it agrees with law and prophets." If the community walks this way of righteousness, it will enter the awaited future kingdom (7:15–27). The Sermon defines "the conditions of entry into the kingdom of God" (217). "Standing or falling in the judgment depends on this praxis."[3]

Guelich does not find Luz's formulation of the relationship of grace and works, of eschatology and ethics convincing. For him the Sermon is primarily a Christological statement, that "Jesus Messiah [is] the one whose coming fulfills the Old Testament promise for the coming of the age of salvation, the coming into history of the Kingdom of Heaven" (27). Jesus proclaims the presence of God's reign, the opportunity to encounter a new relationship with God through "the presence of God's sovereign rule in one's life" (28). This gift of salvation, this display of God's grace and reign in Jesus, this

"Christological indicative," precedes and provides the basis for the Sermon's demands.[4]

"The coming of Jesus Messiah meant . . . a 'messianic community' took shape in the persons of those who responded in faith and followed Jesus." In the beatitudes Jesus announces the eschatological blessings on these ones who "stand before God empty-handed and destitute" (29). The rest of the Sermon outlines conduct commensurate with the new relationship offered by God. "The conduct demanded represents the 'good fruit' of discipleship, not the basis for or the means to achieving discipleship" (31).

But neither is there a "cheap grace" in which disciples receive God's gift without hearing a call to manifest God's gift in their lives. The Sermon's orientation to future judgment, particularly evident in what Hare calls the "Eschatological Epilogue" (7:13–27), addresses this concern.[5] The present life of disciples is lived on the basis of God's gift of grace and in the knowledge and anticipation of their accountability to God in the future judgment and consummation of God's saving activity (38). Faithful discipleship in the present ensures "entrance" to the kingdom at judgment (32). Guelich thus sees a close connection among the Sermon's Christological, ecclesiological, ethical and eschatological dimensions. These aspects constitute the "gospel of the kingdom" which Jesus proclaims (4:23) and which disciples and readers encounter prior to the Sermon (4:17–22). The Sermon elaborates the contours of a way of life commensurate with God's gift and reign.

Thomas Ogletree further discusses the role of eschatology in Matthew's gospel.[6] He argues that Matthew's "dialectical eschatology" identifies the alien nature of the world and refuses to grant ultimacy to it. The eschatology encourages hope, patient waiting and faithful living marked by love in a non-conformist and alternative community "which maintains standards and perceptions different from the dominant society." This community "stands over against the world even as they are situated within it." It holds that the future age is a "substantive reality" in the present. For contemporary Christians Ogletree argues that this eschatology encourages i) some alienation from and critique of "the institutional arrangements of the larger society" and ii) "deep involvement with a community which is engaged in developing qualitatively distinct alternatives to those arrangements." This alternative will affirm the fundamental equality of all people and will participate appropriately in the larger society.[7]

Specific Requirements

Determining the Sermon's specific requirements for the way of life created by the present experience and future anticipation of the reign of God has not always been an easy task for interpreters. We can take one of the six "antithesis" of 5:21–48 as an example, the verses on divorce in 5:31–32.

Commentators have tried to establish how Matthew's late first-century audience may have heard this statement. Matthew's Jesus forbids divorce "except on the ground of unchastity" (5:32). But what does the word translated as "unchastity" in the exceptive clause mean?[8] From study of the word's use in the ancient world, scholars have suggested three possible meanings: fornication (sex prior to marriage), incestuous marriage relationships, adultery. Because verses 31–32 concern marriage, the first possibility does not seem relevant. But most scholars are divided between the two remaining meanings.

John Meier argues that the term refers to incestuous marriage relationships. He points to the strict prohibition in

Jewish traditions on marriages between certain "family" members (see Leviticus 18:6–18). In first-century Judaism, there was debate about what should happen if a Gentile, who was already in one of these marriage relationships, converted to Judaism. Some Jewish teachers required divorce; others understood a new existence to begin which allowed the marriage to continue. The prohibition on divorce in 5:31–32 addresses this problem for Gentiles wanting to be disciples of Jesus in Matthew's community. They must divorce, but this is the only circumstance in which divorce is allowed.[9]

Luz, however, argues that the context of 5:31–32 does not indicate such a restricted meaning for the term. He considers that any link with Leviticus 18 is unlikely because that chapter does not use the central word πορνεία ("unchastity," 5:32). He argues that Deuteronomy 24:1 (cited in 5:31) with its discussion of reasons for divorce indicates the verses' likely focus. They are concerned with ending legitimate, rather than determining illegitimate, marriages. For Luz, the antithesis is to be located in debates within first-century Judaism, especially between the schools of Shammai and Hillel, over how restrictively or widely to interpret the grounds for divorce. Jesus' general prohibition on divorce allies him with the Shammaites.[10] The only situation in which divorce is permitted is that of adultery, an action which renders the marriage impure and which requires its end.[11]

Luz's discussion of these verses explicitly identifies a factor that influences many interpreters. Several times he notes that the confessional tradition of interpreters determines their understanding of the divorce material, especially if they are concerned to uphold a particular view of divorce and remarriage (301, 307). Luz's discussion indicates that it is often impossible to discuss the Sermon's requirements and meaning for its first-century context without, explicitly or implicitly, discussing its meaning for contemporary readers.[12]

The Sermon and Contemporary Readers

Yet the question of how the Sermon addresses contemporary readers is by no means clear. One problem has to do with deciding what sort of material we are reading. For instance, it is common to note that while the first two antitheses deal with internal attitudes and motives (anger, 5:21–25; lust, 5:27–30), the third one focuses on an external action. Some have, accordingly, regarded the antithesis on divorce as providing an enforceable rule for the behavior of any community of disciples. That means that if the word πορνεία ("unchastity") is understood as referring to incestuous marriages as defined by Leviticus 18 and as applied to Gentiles entering the Christian community, then the exceptive clause has little relevance for contemporary communities of faith. The effect of this reading is that divorce is essentially forbidden for contemporary church members. Or if the word is understood as meaning "adultery," then divorce is permissible only after adulterous behavior.

Both scenarios pose some obvious problems for a realistic church discipline that accounts for human frailty, that is shaped by Matthew's concern for mercy (5:7; 9:13; 12:7) and that offers realistic boundaries and guidance for members and ministers of congregations. Luz notes that any attempt to apply 5:32 strictly as a law comes into tension with the center of Jesus' proclamation, "the unconditional love of God for the human being."[13] Yet on the other hand, he recognizes that if churches ignore the antithesis' demand for life-long monogamy, they end up taking "the way of least resistance," having to "accept everything and remain silent in the face of everything," unaware that laws can also "provide help to love."

The challenge is to discover "how the faithfulness in marriage demanded by God remains free without becoming relative" (310). Luz, however, does not offer contemporary disciples ways in which to address this challenge.

One approach to the issue of the Sermon's function for contemporary hearers has been to consider the type of language found in the Sermon. For example, with respect to the exceptive clause in the divorce statement (5:31–32), Hare seems to understand the key term πορνεία (adultery) to mean for contemporary readers not only infidelity but also "neglect, abuse, failure to communicate or simply unresolved tensions regarding reciprocal expectations." In such situations "the marriage is no longer real"; divorce is a "positive step."[14]

In an influential article, Robert Tannehill considers the type of language found in the antitheses.[15] Taking as his starting point the fifth antithesis on retaliation (5:39–42), he argues that recognizing the metaphorical nature of the language is crucial if we are to "bespeak the message of the original text in a new situation" (374).

The antithesis is introduced by a general principle ("Do not resist one who is evil," 5:39a) which is followed by four specific and extreme commands:

Turn the other cheek
Let the person have your cloak
Go two miles
Give to the one who begs from you.

The four specific and extreme commands identify concrete situations, yet "we take them as examples which are relevant to many situations which have nothing to do with cheeks and coats and forced service" (377–78).[16] How we are able to do this is the focus of Tannehill's analysis.

One factor has to do with the "specificness" of the four commands. While they require certain behavior in very concrete situations, Tannehill notes that the presence of a *series* of commands ensures that each command is not restricted to its specific scenario. The series of commands establishes a pattern which can be extended to other instances (378); the language is specific yet "open-ended."

The "extremeness" of the demands is also a key aspect of this pattern. Each instance "stands in deliberate tension with the way [people] normally live and think" (379). This tension "gives the metaphor its power to point beyond the literal sense of the words . . . [and to] point the hearer beyond the literal sense to the many situations" in which the hearer encounters other people (380). The antithesis is a "focal instance" within a much larger field of reference.

A further key element in the language's function is its impact on hearers. The extreme language shocks and provokes. The hearer's "mouth falls open" and we immediately engage in self-justification and protection of our way of being (379–80). Yet the specific and extreme language

> arouses the moral imagination, enabling the hearers to see their situation in a new way and to contemplate new possibilities of action. . . . The focal instance serves as an illuminator of the hearer's situation. The hearer is invited to lay the saying alongside [the hearer's] own situation and, through the imaginative shock produced, to see that situation in a new way. (382–83)

For Tannehill, the open-ended nature of the language of the "focal instance" which engages the hearer's "moral imagination" is a key aspect of its ability to speak to situations that are far beyond that of the time of the Sermon's origin.[17] While Tannehill's discussion centers on the antitheses of

5:21–48, his observations about the function of metaphorical language have significance for much of the language of the Sermon.

Richard Horsley also considers how the "non-retaliation" and "love for enemies" antitheses (5:38–48) might address contemporary readers.[18] Horsley begins by recognizing that these verses have often been interpreted to support "traditional Christian pacifism" (3). Among recent writers, Martin Hengel, John Yoder and Stanley Hauerwas have argued for such an interpretation.[19] Yet, though conceding that he himself is a pacifist and practitioner of non-violence (27, footnote 15), Horsley argues that for the first-century hearers of the Sermon these verses (5:38–42) "pertain neither to external, political enemies nor to the question of non-violence or non-resistance" (3). They refer to a local situation of conflict with persecutors who are not Romans[20] or an exploitative ruling class, but a group outside the Matthean community. Members of the Matthean community, the hearers of the Sermon, are called to take social and economic responsibility for others in their local residential community who, like them, suffer from economically oppressive behavior. They are to extend mercy even to those who are their enemies, thereby realizing God's will (22–24).[21]

Horsley asks whether these verses have any relevance for the ethics of contemporary readers. He considers four ways in which scholars have linked scripture and ethics, indicating briefly how each approach might work with 5:38–48.[22] One method emphasizes "character development [in which] the Bible provides contemporary ethical agents with paradigms of disposition, intention and action that inform their manner of life." On this basis, these antitheses would require hearers to form alternative economic and social structures when existing ones fail to sustain adequate living (24–25).[23] A second approach calls for a faithful remembering and appropriation of the story of Jesus by communities of faith. Careful hearing of the story of Jesus may require a critical evaluation of the readers' present situation (including a naming of "enemies") as the starting point for a faithful lifestyle.[24] A third way is to identify analogies between the "particular events, issues and set of relationships" in the text and the interpreter's own situation. Such an approach requires self-critique and a comprehensive analysis of any contemporary situation that might be deemed analogous (25–26).[25] A fourth approach "broadens the implications and applications of the Jesus sayings into universal ethical rules or ideals" such as love (27). To universalize the material requires taking into account the concern of the sayings with social-economic realities. To "love" could include, for instance, "the use of economic resources for the benefit for the needy and oppressed."

In an influential article, James Gustafson offers a fifth possibility for "the place of scripture in Christian ethics."[26] Gustafson argues that instead of using scripture as "moral law, moral ideals or the source of moral analogies" (454), scripture provides a significant but not exclusive resource for the believing community as it seeks to "discern what God is enabling and requiring [people] to be and do in particular natural, historical and social circumstances." The scriptures, with all their "great variety of moral values, moral norms and principles and many different kinds of literature . . . are not reducible to a single theme." Out of this great diversity, the scriptures function to inform the moral judgments of the community as it engages in "reflective discourse about present events in the light of appeals to this variety of material [in the scriptures] as well as to other principles and experiences" (444). In this approach, the contents of Matthew's Sermon (or any part of scripture) are not sufficient on their own to supply all the guidance that a community needs.

Rather the Sermon interfaces with the particular circumstances and issues of a community of faith and with the continuing Christian tradition (444–45). The Sermon is a voice in a dialogical and reflective process whereby "persons and communities as finite moral agents responsible to God" determine what God is enabling and requiring them to do and be (455).[27]

Whether one sees the Sermon providing i) paradigms of the attitudes, actions and character required of disciples, ii) ingredients of the informing story, iii) analogies with the present situation, iv) universal principles, or v) a resource for a congregation's reflective discourse on its lifestyle in actual circumstances, it is clear that these five approaches take seriously the Sermon's content. They offer a range of ways by which to understand its lifestyle-shaping and identity-forming power for *communities* of disciples.[28]

The Sermon's Informing Content

Given such a function for the Sermon, scholars have continued to work at identifying important aspects of the Sermon's content. Lisa Cahill summarizes contemporary discussions.[29]

Cahill follows Guelich in seeing the presence of the kingdom of heaven as the "subject of the Sermon" (149). Its presence is evident in "converted relationship" and action from those who have encountered its presence in Jesus. The new relationship with God which Jesus makes possible enables individuals to transform relationships so that they become "doers of concrete actions concerned foremost with . . . meeting the needs of others they affect" (148). The "imitation of God" forms a key element in shaping these actions. Like God, the disciple is merciful (5:7), loves indiscriminately (5:44–45), is perfect (5:48), and forgives (6:12, 14–15). "Righteousness in God's eyes is not purity and lawabidingness, but mercifulness effective in compassionate actions" (150). The theme of righteous action is paired with that of judgment in chapter 7 to warn disciples of the consequences of falling short by reminding them of their accountability to God.

Cahill also considers "the roles and responsibilities of the disciple as also a member of communities whose identity is not primarily religious" (152–53). She notes that the Sermon's emphasis on "active, personal outflow of a total conversion," on "individual commitment within a supportive community . . . does not suggest a "social ethics" in any direct or usual sense" (152–53).

But even if "the Sermon does not plainly dictate social objectives, it may imply them." Cahill draws out some implications of the Sermon's demand for inclusive mercy. "One can hardly forgive another, show mercy in the face of his or her need, and treat the other as oneself would want to be treated, if the other is perceived as alien and approached in terms of gender, race, national, religious and class stereotypes." Such mercy requires solidarity with the oppressed (Hendrickx) and non-violent response to evil (Yoder). The Sermon's definition of discipleship as an existence pervaded by the imitation of God presents insights which "challenge secular society" and call disciples to such action (153–56).

The Sermon and Social Context

Other interpreters are more insistent on the community-forming impact of the Sermon and its demand for social transformation. In delineating aspects of the communal lifestyle created through interaction with the Sermon, interpreters are very much shaped by their own social location and issues.

For instance, several German commentators writing in

the 1980's identify the issue of peace and the threat of nuclear annihilation as an important context for their interpretation of the Sermon and as a significant area of its contemporary address. Strecker suggests that the sense of "total threat to existence" creates an existential analogy of "atmosphere and reality" between contemporary readers of the Sermon and its first-century audience. In this context, its call to love even the enemy (5:44; 7:12) mandates a way of life necessary for human survival.[30] The New Zealand writer Ray Galvin, whose country declared itself a nuclear-free zone in the 1980's and thereby excluded the nuclear-powered and armed ships of the United States from its ports, also finds the Sermon to address the situation of nuclear threat.[31] Martin Luther King cited the Sermon's demand for love as a foundation for the civil rights movement's strategy of non-violent protest.[32] Eric Lott has pursued the meaning of the Sermon in the context of Christians in India and in relation to the legacy of Mahatma Gandhi. He notes that

> discussion of this text in the West has unfortunately tended to remain at the level of discussing the precise theoretical status of the Sermon's ethical demands, rather than move on to interpret these ethical implications in a more inclusive vision of faith's life-style.[33]

Michael Crosby has sought in several books to elucidate the Sermon's contribution to social justice concerns for first-world Christians.[34] As a "liberation theologian" he adopts the method of Latin American theologian Juan Luis Segundo. This method begins with experience that jars one's present values and behavior. With reflection, suspicion grows about one's present experience and understanding of reality including God. This suspicion leads to a rereading of the Bible and to the formation of new understanding about God, the world and faith. This new understanding requires a faithful carrying out of God's will.

Crosby reads the beatitudes and Lord's Prayer with the central realization that this world in its individual, interpersonal, institutional and ideological forms "stands in direct opposition to God's plan for creation." It is a world marked by oppression, bondage and social injustice. From this perspective, Crosby finds in the Sermon a different reality centered in a community that does the will of God. This will is the justice or reign of God which can transform every aspect of current social and economic structures.[35] Hence Crosby wants to hear the Sermon's address to readers who share this context and are thereby participants in its unjust socio-economic and political structures.

Crosby's larger study, *House of Disciples*, examines "the ecclesial and economic dimensions of Matthew's notion of justice and how these justice dimensions touch upon" contemporary ethics, spirituality, economics and ecclesiology (1). Crosby argues "that Matthew's reordering of the house—be it church-order or economics (house-order)—demands justice at its core. This justice can be identified as the salvific (re)ordering of relationships with God and others, as well as the socio-political (re)ordering of resources not only in the house church, but throughout the world and throughout the earth itself" (2–3, 146). This right-ordering of relationships and resources in household units involves equality of relationship in place of authoritative, patriarchal hierarchy. It requires general reciprocity and the sharing of resources among all instead of structures which maintain one's own status and inequitable distribution (99–125).

In this context, the Sermon articulates "variations on a basic structure of justice" (181). The word "justice" (δικαιοσύνη, also translated "righteousness") appears five times in the Sermon (5:6, 10, 20; 6:1, 33).

> Experiencing the saving power of God's δικαιοσύνη (5:6; 6:33) brings about the blessing, the fulfillment of God's plan of salvation. Members of the community are to witness to this saving act of God's justice by their own acts of justice (5:10, 20; 6:1).[36]

"Justice" provides the principle which shapes the Sermon's structure. The beatitudes (5:3–16) outline the blessed way of life in which relationships and resources are reordered (170). In verses 17–48 of chapter 5, fulfilling the Torah takes place as "households . . . fulfill the salvific and economic elements of justice" (182). Justice is also realized "through deeds performed for God to see" (6:1–32) and "in right relations with others and God" (6:33–7:12; 152–95).

In Crosby's analysis, the Sermon identifies what is to be the central commitment of the church. Following Hauerwas, he argues that "the church does not have a social ethic; the church is a social ethic" (143). The basis of this alternative community is the presence of God's reign. "This membership in God's reign will be realized through house churches of dedicated disciples (now as then) who act responsibly." The demand to do God's will

> makes us one family. This notion offers an insight that is applicable to today's ecclesiastical and economic problems, especially those related to the dignity of persons in the church and economy and to the distribution of resources—be that distribution in the form of roles or material goods.[37]

Other liberation theologians have interacted with the Sermon in very different contexts but have seen a similar emphasis on justice and on the creation of an alternative community, the church. Hendrickx' reading of the Sermon reflects the influence of his experience in the Philippines. Noting the importance of the "kingdom" or reign of God in the context and content of the Sermon (4:17, 23; 5:3, 10; 6:10), he writes:

> The kingdom of God means, then, to identify with people, especially the threatened, the oppressed and the downtrodden; to give life to those who have none; to remove the oppressive relationships of one person over another, or one nation over another, to bring them to mutual solidarity; to liberate people from any kind of fear . . . [38]

The Peruvian priest and theologian Gustavo Gutiérrez also understands the presence of the kingdom of God to be central to the Sermon (6:33).[39] The Sermon is concerned with discipleship as the community of disciples incarnates God's gift and demand in its daily social existence (118–39). Hence Gutiérrez rejects any reading of the beatitudes that spiritualizes them. "The beatitudes in Matthew therefore are the Magna Carta of the congregation. . . . Our following in his footsteps finds expression in actions toward our neighbor, especially the poor, in life-giving works" (118). Gutiérrez, along with another Latin American scholar Elsa Tamez, underlines the importance of the opening beatitude (5:3) in declaring God's identification with the poor.[40]

Segundo Galilea, a Catholic priest from Chile, reads the beatitudes in relation to the church's "deepest identity" as a community of evangelization.[41] This task and identity of evangelization derives from and leads to Jesus Christ; it is incarnational, transformative, liberating and directed primarily to those who are marginalized (1–3, 52–53). The beatitudes provide "an indispensable guide to evangelization" because they offer "first and foremost a message about Christ and his kingdom. The Beatitudes reveal what God is, not just what we should be. They teach us what the kingdom of God is, and not just what we must do in order to enter it. . . . Evangelization must be faithful to the truth about Jesus, faithful to the truth about the kingdom, and faithful to the imitation of Christ the evangelizer" (9–10).[42]

For Galilea, the first beatitude requires an "evangelical poverty—that is, interior liberty as expressed in a concrete and social lifestyle" marked by a "predilection for the poor" (37–39). The third and fourth beatitudes indicate that to "evangelize means to produce human beings who are 'just' and who in turn will ardently desire the propagation of this justice all about them" (48). "The justice and holiness of the kingdom, both as grace and as requirement, begins with a conversion of the heart, a personal change." But it also has a social dimension which opposes "social sinfulness" and demands from the church "toil for justice . . . service to the poor and commitment to their integral liberation" (46–47). "The reason for the social dimension of evangelization, then, is that, in order to create a communion of brothers and sisters in the world, one must deliver that world from its social servitude, from its social sinfulness—as this is expressed in economics, politics and culture" (54). Such is the task of the community of the merciful (52–53) and the peacemakers (75). This way of life, this identity of the Christian community can only be sustained by prayer (5:8; 70–74). But also it is a way of life that leads "us to the highest degree of identification with Jesus: persecution and martyrdom." That is the price for those whose "commitments and involvements go contrary to the interests of human beings and their unjust sinful society" (83, 87).

Conclusion

In chapters 4 and 5 we have explored some of the contemporary debate about the content of the Sermon. Though for convenience we have divided the material between more theoretical and practical concerns, it should be clear that the Sermon does not endorse such a division. Yet though the Sermon demands a distinct way of life from the community of disciples, we have seen that interpreters do not agree on what this lifestyle looks like. Their disagreement stems to some degree from their different ways of understanding the Sermon's presentation of Christian existence and the interaction of aspects such as grace, demand and eschatology. Also impacting the diverse interpretations are their differing understandings of how biblical texts can shape contemporary ethics and what methods should be employed for this task. In part the disagreement reflects the very different social locations, experiences and issues of the interpreters as they enter into dialogue with the Sermon and each other. Yet underlying this diversity of content, method, and context, there is the conviction of the necessity of engagement with this significant text in the Christian tradition.

Notes

1. Luz, *Matthew*, 214–15; Davies and Allison, *Matthew*, 440, 720; Guelich, *Sermon on the Mount*, 27–33; Lapide, *Sermon*, 3–10. See also the survey of interpretations cited throughout Luz's discussion and in Schweizer, *Good News*, 193–209.

2. For instance, Charles Carlston ("Matthew 6:24–34," *Interpretation* 41 [1987] 179–83) raises the question about this passage. See also Hendrickx, "The Practicability of the Sermon on the Mount," in *Sermon on the Mount*, 177–83; Lambrecht, *Sermon on the Mount*, 20–24, 74–77, 106–17, 198–204; Frederick Schuele, "Living Up to Matthew's Sermon on the Mount: An

Approach," in *Christian Biblical Ethics* (ed. Robert J. Daly; New York: Paulist, 1984) 200–210; Luz, *Matthew 1–7*, 456–60.

3. Also Strecker, *Sermon*, 33–34.

4. Also Hamm, *Beatitudes*, 110–14; Davies and Allison, *Matthew*, 427, 440; Hendrickx, *Sermon*, 181–83. See the somewhat different formulation of Mohrlang, *Matthew and Paul*, 78–81. Donald Capps ("The Beatitudes and Erikson's Life Cycle Theory," *Pastoral Psychology* 33 [1985] 226–44, esp. 232–33) recognizes the transforming presence of the kingdom in the present age.

5. Hare, *Matthew*, 81.

6. Thomas Ogletree, *The Use of the Bible in Christian Ethics* (Philadelphia: Fortress, 1983) 177–92; also Mohrlang, *Matthew and Paul*, 48–57. Guelich (*Sermon*, 19–20) recognizes that it was Albert Schweitzer who emphasized the significance of the Sermon's eschatological perspective.

7. For discussion of the relationship of eschatology and ethics, see, for example, Amos Wilder, *Eschatology and Ethics in the Teaching of Jesus* (Rev. Ed.; New York: Harper, 1950); Rudolf Schnackenburg, "The Sermon on the Mount and Modern Man," *Christian Existence*, 128–57, esp. 146–47; J. Christiaan Beker, "The Challenge of Paul's Apocalyptic Gospel for the Church Today," *Journal of Religious Thought* 40 (1983) 9–15; C. Freeman Sleeper (*The Bible and Moral Life* [Louisville: Westminster/John Knox, 1992] 66–82, 163–64) argues that apocalyptic thinking i) maintains a sense of urgency which spurs the church to action, ii) emphasizes purity which reminds the church to guard its identity in a secular world, and iii) relativizes worldly power with its focus on divine sovereignty.

8. Both RSV and NRSV translate the Greek word πορνεία as "unchastity." The New Jerusalem Bible translates it as "an illicit marriage" (see the discussion of Meier below), while the New International Version prefers "marital unfaithfulness."

9. Meier, *Law and History in Matthew's Gospel*, 140–50; idem, *Vision of Matthew*, 248–57; Joseph Bonsirven, *Le divorce dans le Nouveau Testament* (Tournai: Desclee, 1948); Heinrich Baltensweiler, "Die Ehebruchsklauseln bei Matthaus. Zu Matth. 5,32; 19,9," *TZ* 15 (1959) 340–56; Joseph Fitzmyer, "The Matthean Divorce Texts and Some New Palestinian Evidence," *TS* 37 (1976) 197–226.

10. This view is opposed by Samuel Lachs, *A Rabbinic Commentary on the New Testament. The Gospels of Matthew, Mark and Luke* (Hoboken: Ktav, 1987) 99.

11. Luz, *Matthew*, 298–310; Davies and Allison, *Matthew*, 527–32; Strecker, *Sermon on the Mount*, 72–76; Guelich, *Sermon*, 206; Gundry, *Matthew*, 89–91; James Houlden, *Ethics and the New Testament* (Harmondsworth: Penguin, 1973) 78–79.

12. See the reflection of W. Countryman, *Dirt, Sex and Greed: Sexual Ethics in the New Testament and Their Implications for Today* (Philadelphia: Fortress, 1988) Introduction, chapters 8, 9, 12.

13. Waetjen (*Origin and Destiny*, 98) takes a similar approach. Jesus annuls a law that "does not contribute to the human being's realization of union and wholeness."

14. Hare, *Matthew*, 54.

15. Robert Tannehill, "The 'Focal Instance' as a Form of New Testament Speech: A Study of Matthew 5:39b–42," *Journal of Religion* 50 (1970) 372–85. See also Schnackenburg, "Sermon on the Mount," 149–50.

16. Luz (*Matthew 1–7*, 335–37) argues similarly that the fifth and sixth antitheses "were meant not as law but as examples and with the intent of leaving . . . room for creative fancy." The specific situation and the demand for love are crucial elements for this continuing reflection. Guelich (*Sermon*, 263–65) also rejects any legalistic implementation of their demands.

17. It should be noted that Tannehill ("The 'Focal Instance,' "
    380–81) contrasts the language of the "focal instance" with
    that of the "legal rule" as exemplified by the divorce antithesis
    in 5:31–32. But one could argue (Luz, *Matthew*, 309–10) that
    the language of 5:31–32 functions in the same way. Finding
    coherent connections among the various aspects also engages
    the reader's "moral imagination." See Wolfgang Iser, *The Act
    of Reading* (Baltimore: Johns Hopkins, 1978).

18. Richard A. Horsley, "Ethics and Exegesis: 'Love Your Ene-
    mies' and the Doctrine of Non-Violence," *JAAR* 54 (1986) 3–
    31.

19. Martin Hengel, *Was Jesus a Revolutionist?* (FBBS 28; Philadel-
    phia: Fortress, 1971) 26–29; John Yoder, "The Political Axi-
    oms of the Sermon on the Mount," in *The Original Revolution*
    (Scottdale: Herald, 1971) 46–49; Stanley Hauerwas, *The
    Peaceable Kingdom* (Notre Dame: University of Notre Dame,
    1983) xxiv, Chapters 5–6. See also William Klassen, *Love of
    Enemies* (Philadelphia: Fortress, 1984) chapter 4; Stephen C.
    Mott, *Biblical Ethics and Social Change* (New York: Oxford
    University, 1982) chapter 9. For a different position, Walter
    Wink, "Beyond Just War and Pacifism: Jesus' Nonviolent
    Way," *Review and Expositor* 89 (1992) 197–214. For a review
    of Christian thinking about war, in which these antitheses have
    had a prominent place, see Lisa Cahill, "Nonresistance, De-
    fense, Violence and the Kingdom in Christian Tradition," *In-
    terpretation* 38 (1984) 380–97; C. John Cadoux, *The Early
    Christian Attitude to War* (New York: Seabury, 1982); Roland
    H. Bainton, *Christian Attitudes to War and Peace* (New York:
    Abingdon, 1960).

20. Horsley rejects the argument of John Yoder (*The Politics of
    Jesus* [Grand Rapids: Eerdmans, 1972] 43–47, 56; idem, *Origi-
    nal Revolution*, 21–24) and M. Hengel (*Victory over Violence*
    [Philadelphia: Fortress, 1973] 49–50, Fn 101) that Jesus' advo-
    cacy of non-violence is in opposition to the Zealots' military
    option. Davies and Allison (*Matthew 1–7*, 551) understand

"enemies" as "those who persecute Christians." So also Gundry, *Matthew*, 97 and Luz, *Matthew 1–7*, 343 (though a reference to "national enemies in a war" is "by no means" excluded). Guelich (*Sermon*, 227–9) sees the reference to persecution arising particularly from mission, and embracing those who reject "God's redemption activity." Hare (*Matthew*, 58–60) identifies a more inclusive reference embracing personal, national and "class" (racial, sexist or economic oppressors) enemies.

21. In her analysis, Luise Schottroff ("Non-Violence and the Love of One's Enemies," in *Essays on the Love Commandment* [Tr. Reginald and Ilse Fuller; Philadelphia: Fortress, 1978] 9–39) emphasizes that "love of enemy" is not "general humanitarian love" which can be abstracted from particular social structures and circumstances, but is the behavior "expected of Christians when they encounter resistance" (13).

22. William C. Spohn (*What Are They Saying About Scripture and Ethics?* [New York: Paulist, 1984]) identifies six approaches.

23. This approach has been advocated by James Gustafsen, "The Relation of the Gospels to Moral Life," in *Theology and Christian Ethics* (Philadelphia: Pilgrim, 1974) 147–59. The formation of character has also been emphasized by Stanley Hauerwas, *A Community of Character* (Notre Dame: University of Notre Dame, 1981).

24. See, especially Hauerwas, *Community of Character*; also *Peaceable Kingdom*.

25. See James M. Gustafson, "The Place of Scripture in Christian Ethics: A Methodological Study," *Interpretation* 24 (1970) 430–55, esp. 442–43.

26. Gustafson, "The Place of Scripture in Christian Ethics."

27. Gustafson ("Place of Scripture," 444–45) readily recognizes the "looseness" of this approach and warns against predetermining one's position and then finding biblical support for it.

28. The communal address of the Sermon is consonant with a more widespread recognition in discussions of biblical ethics that biblical texts primarily address communities of disciples, rather than individuals. For instance, see John Yoder, "Let the Church be the Church," in *Original Revolution*, 107–24; idem, "The Hermeneutics of Peoplehood: A Protestant Perspective," in *The Priestly Kingdom: Social Ethics as Gospel* (Notre Dame: University of Notre Dame, 1984) 15–45; Hauerwas, *Community of Character*; idem, *Peaceable Kingdom*; Mott, "The Church as Counter-Community," in *Biblical Ethics*, 128–41; Ogletree, *The Use of the Bible*; Allen Verhey, *The Great Reversal* (Grand Rapids: Eerdmans, 1984) chapter 4; Bruce Birch and Larry Rasmussen, *Bible and Ethics in the Christian Life* (Rev. and Expanded; Minneapolis: Augsburg Fortress, 1989) chapters 2, 7; Stephen Fowl and Gregory Jones, *Reading in Communion: Scripture and Ethics in Christian Life* (Grand Rapids: Eerdmans, 1991). Also Luz, *Matthew 1–7*, 456–58.

29. Lisa Cahill, "The Ethical Implications of the Sermon on the Mount," *Interpretation* 41 (1987) 144–56. See also Yoder, "The Political Axioms of the Sermon on the Mount," in *Original Revolution*, 34–51; Richard Lischer, "The Sermon on the Mount as Radical Pastoral Care," *Interpretation* 41 (1987) 157–69; Eduard Lohse, *Theological Ethics of the New Testament* (Minneapolis: Fortress, 1991) 61–73. For a fine discussion of ethics in the gospel of Matthew, Leander Keck, "Ethics in the Gospel According to Matthew," *Iliff Review* 40 (1984) 39–56; also Wolfgang Schrage, *The Ethics of the New Testament* (Philadelphia: Fortress, 1988) 143–52.

30. Strecker, *Sermon*, 181–85; Luz, *Matthew 1–7*, 458–60; Franz Alt *(Peace is Possible: The Politics of the Sermon on the Mount* [New York: Schocken Books, 1985] 86, 103) writes, "The Sermon on the Mount and nuclear missiles are incompatible." He proposes that humans must choose the Sermon's call for love or face the "End of History" (105).

31. Ray Galvin, *The Peace of Christ in a Nuclear Age* (Auckland: G. W. Moore, 1983) 58–59.

32. See the sermon on Mt 5:43–48 "Loving your enemies," Martin Luther King, *Strength to Love* (Philadelphia: Fortress, 1963, 1981) 47–55.

33. Eric Lott, "The Indian Christian and the Sermon on the Mount," *Bangalore Theological Forum* 17 (1985) 1–8.

34. Michael Crosby, *Thy Will be Done: Praying the Our Father as Subversive Activity* (Maryknoll: Orbis, 1977); idem, *Spirituality of the Beatitudes* (Maryknoll: Orbis, 1981); idem, *House of Disciples: Church, Economics and Justice in Matthew* (Maryknoll: Orbis, 1988).

35. Crosby, *Spirituality*, chaps. 1–2; idem, *House of Disciples*, 142–46, 229–67; idem, *Thy Will*, 1–20.

36. Crosby, *House of Disciples*, 181.

37. Crosby, *House of Disciples*, 143–44.

38. Hendrickx, *Sermon on the Mount*, 1–3, 177–83.

39. Gustavo Gutiérrez, *The God of Life* (Maryknoll: Orbis, 1989, 1991) 103–05.

40. Elsa Tamez, *Bible of the Oppressed* (Maryknoll: Orbis, 1982) 72–74; Gustavo Gutiérrez, *A Theology of Liberation* (Maryknoll: Orbis, 1973, 1988) 162–73, esp. 169–71.

41. Segundo Galilea, *The Beatitudes: To Evangelize as Jesus Did* (Maryknoll, New York: Orbis, 1984).

42. John P. Meier ("Matthew 5:3–12," *Interpretation* 44 [1990] 281–85) also reads the Beatitudes as primarily a witness to the identity of Jesus, "a perfect self-portrait by the Master" (285).

Conclusion

Our survey of some of the scholarly discussion about
Matthew's Sermon on the Mount indicates that they are saying many and various things about the Sermon. If we are
looking for an easy or simple answer to the question posed
by this book's title, this observation will disappoint and frus-
trate us. I would suggest, however, that this diversity has an
extremely positive dimension. It bears witness to the depth
and richness of current scholarship on the Sermon, to the
complexity and profundity of the material being interpreted,
and to the open-ended nature of the interpretive task itself.

It is possible, however, to identify a central concern
flowing through the present debates. As we noted in chapter
4, Jeremias identified this concern in 1960 as, "What is the
meaning of the Sermon?" Our discussion of scholarship from
the last thirty years or so indicates that the question must be
rephrased a little: "What are the meanings of the Sermon?"
The "meaning" of the Sermon is polyvalent. The answers
will depend on where an interpreter stands and what particular questions an interpreter asks. That is, our discussion has
highlighted the importance of method, focus and social location in the interpretive process.

One way of trying to answer our rephrased question has

been to understand the "composing," the putting-together of the Sermon, with regard both to its sources and to its structure (chapters 1–2). How sources are interpreted and how material is organized in the final form of a document shine light on the question of meaning.

Another approach to the question of the Sermon's meaning has been to focus on the specific situation of the community for whom Matthew's Sermon was shaped and to whom it was addressed (chapter 3). Scholars have tried to identify the experiences and issues of Matthew's readers to understand the Sermon's function in that context. That is, these approaches have focused on more historical answers to the question of the Sermon's meaning.

Further, scholars have recognized that the Sermon cannot be separated from its present location as part of Matthew's gospel. Its meaning is impacted not only by understanding how the sections of chapters 5–7 cohere with each other, not only by unraveling the nuances of its content, but also by the presentations of Jesus (Christology) and discipleship (ecclesiology) that precede and follow it. This approach has concentrated more on literary and theological answers (chapters 4–5).

Finally, as chapter 5 in particular indicates, some scholars are very aware that the question of the meanings of the Sermon cannot be answered "objectively" by the text alone. Rather, answers will be shaped not only by the text but also by the impact of the interpreters' social context on the interpretive process. Different social locations lead interpreters to pose diverse questions as they engage the Sermon. Out of this engagement shaped by particular circumstances and experiences come different understandings of the Sermon. For some interpreters the answer to the question of the Sermon's meaning is, ultimately, a matter of a particular way of life and self-understanding lived in a specific social context.

What will they be saying about Matthew's Sermon on the Mount in thirty years' time? I would hazard to suggest two possible areas of interest. One involves literary approaches to the Sermon. As we noted in chapter 1, redaction criticism's concern with the sources and shaping of the Sermon is increasingly giving way in gospel studies to a focus on the finished form of the text and to the interaction between text and reader. Our survey shows minimal work on the Sermon from this perspective to date.

A second guess would be that we will see readings of the Sermon that are concerned explicitly with its meaning in relation to particular social locations such as third world settings, women, and mainline churches in increasingly minority social locations. I suspect that such readings will counter "individualized" western readings of the Sermon by emphasizing a communitarian understanding of discipleship, calling readers to live in some tension with the norms and values of the surrounding society because God's saving presence is among the community of disciples (Mt 1:23). Such readings will continue the long discussion of the Sermon's ethical meaning with reference to new circumstances.

For Further Reading

Commentaries on Matthew

Albright, W. F. and C. S. Mann, *Matthew*. Anchor Bible 26; Garden City, New York: Doubleday, 1971.

Davies, W. D. and Dale Allison. *The Gospel According to Saint Matthew* Vol. 1. ICC; Edinburgh: T. & T. Clark, 1988.

Gundry, Robert. *Matthew: A Commentary on His Literary and Theological Art*. Grand Rapids: Eerdmans, 1982.

Hare, Douglas R. A. *Matthew*. Interpretation; Louisville: John Knox, 1993

Harrington, Daniel. *The Gospel of Matthew*. Sacra Pagina; Collegeville: Liturgical, 1991.

Hill, David. *The Gospel of Matthew*. NCB; Grand Rapids/ London: Eerdmans, Marshall Morgan & Scott, 1972.

Luz, Ulrich. *Matthew 1–7*. Minneapolis: Augsburg, 1989.

Patte, Daniel. *The Gospel According to Matthew: A Structural Commentary on Matthew's Faith*. Philadelphia: Fortress, 1987.

Schweizer, Eduard. *The Good News According to Matthew*. Atlanta: John Knox, 1975.

Waetjen, Herman. *The Origin and Destiny of Humanness*. Corte Madera, CA: Omega, 1976.

Commentaries on the Sermon on the Mount

Guelich, Robert. *The Sermon on the Mount: A Foundation for Understanding*. Dallas: Word, 1982.

Hendrickx, Herman. *The Sermon on the Mount*. London: Geoffrey Chapman, 1984.

Lambrecht, Jan. *The Sermon on the Mount: Proclamation and Exhortation*. Good News Studies, 14; Wilmington: Michael Glazier, 1985.

Lapide, Pinchas. *The Sermon on the Mount*. Maryknoll: Orbis, 1986.

Strecker, Georg. *The Sermon on the Mount*. Nashville: Abingdon, 1988.

Book Discussions

Balch, David, ed. *Social History of the Matthean Community*. Minneapolis: Augsburg, 1991.

Bellinzoni, Arthur J., ed. *The Two-Source Hypothesis*. Macon: Mercer University, 1985.

Betz, Hans D. *Essays on the Sermon on the Mount*. Philadelphia: Fortress, 1985.

Bornkamm, Günther, Gerhard Barth and Heinz Joachim Held. *Tradition and Interpretation in Matthew*. London: SCM, 1963, 1971.

Brooks, Stephenson, H. *Matthew's Community: The Evidence of His Special Sayings Material*. Sheffield: Sheffield Academic, 1987.

Crosby, Michael. *House of Disciples: Church, Economics and Justice in Matthew*. Maryknoll: Orbis, 1988.

————. *Thy Will Be Done: Praying The Our Father As Subversive Activity*. Maryknoll: Orbis, 1977.

————. *Spirituality Of The Beatitudes*. Maryknoll: Orbis, 1981.

Davies, W. D. *The Setting of the Sermon on the Mount*. Cambridge: Cambridge University, 1963.

Donaldson, Terence. *Jesus on the Mountain: A Study in Matthean Theology*. JSNTSS 8; Sheffield: University of Sheffield, 1985.

Farmer, William. *The Synoptic Problem: A Critical Analysis*. New York: Macmillan, 1964.

Galilea, Segundo. *The Beatitudes. To Evangelize as Jesus Did*. Maryknoll: Orbis, 1984.

Goulder, Michael. *Midrash and Lection in Matthew*. London: SPCK, 1974.

Gutiérrez, Gustavo. *The God of Life*. Maryknoll: Orbis, 1989, 1991.

Hamm, Dennis. *The Beatitudes in Context*. Wilmington: Michael Glazier, 1990.

Hare, Douglas. *The Theme of Jewish Persecution of Christians in the Gospel According to St. Matthew*. SNTSMS 6; Cambridge: Cambridge University, 1967.

Jeremias, Joachim. *The Sermon on the Mount*. FBBS: Philadelphia: Fortress, 1963.

Kilpatrick, G. D. *The Origins of the Gospel According to St. Matthew*. London: Oxford University, 1946.

Kingsbury, Jack D. *Matthew as Story*. Philadelphia: Fortress, 1986.

Meier, John P. *Law and History in Matthew's Gospel: A Redactional Study of Mt. 5:17–48*. Analecta Biblica 71; Rome: Biblical Institute, 1976.

————, *The Vision of Matthew: Christ, Church and Morality in the First Gospel*. Theological Inquiries; New York: Paulist, 1979.

Ogletree, Thomas. *The Use of the Bible in Christian Ethics*. Philadelphia: Fortress, 1983.

Schweizer, Eduard, *Matthäus und Seine Gemeinde*. SBS 71. Stuttgart: KBW, 1974.

Senior, Donald. *What Are They Saying About Matthew?* New York: Paulist, 1983.

Stanton, Graham. *A Gospel For a New People: Studies in Matthew*. Edinburgh: T & T Clark, 1992.

————, ed. *The Interpretation of Matthew*. Philadelphia: SPCK and Fortress, 1983.

Streeter, Burton H. *The Four Gospels*. New York: Macmillan, 1925.

Articles

Allison, Dale. "A New Approach to the Sermon on the Mount," *Eph Th L* 64 (1988) 405–14.

————. "The Structure of the Sermon on the Mount," *JBL* 106 (1987) 423–45.

Banks, Robert J. "Matthew's Understanding of the Law; Authenticity and Reinterpretation in Matthew 5:17–20," *JBL* 93 (1974) 226–42.

Betz, Hans D. "The Sermon on the Mount in Matthew's Interpretation," *The Future of Early Christianity: Essays in Honor of Helmut Koester*. Ed. B. A. Pearson. Minneapolis: Fortress, 1991, 258–75.

Bornkamm, Günther. "Der Aufbau der Bergpredigt," *NTS* 24 (1977–78) 419–32.

Brown, Raymond. "The Pater Noster as an Eschatological Prayer," *New Testament Essays*. New York: Paulist, 1965, 1982. 217–53.

Cahill, Lisa. "The Ethical Implications of the Sermon on the Mount," *Interpretation* 38 1984, 380–97.

Carlston, Charles. "Betz on the Sermon on the Mount," *CBQ* 50 (1988) 47–57.

————. "Recent American Interpretation of the Sermon on the Mount," *Bangalore Theological Forum* XVII (1985) 9–22.

Fitzmyer, Joseph A. "The Priority of Mark and the "Q" Source in Luke," *Jesus and Man's Hope*, ed. Donald Miller. Perspective: Pittsburgh Theological Seminary, 1970. Vol. 1, 131–70.

Guelich, Robert. "Interpreting the Sermon on the Mount," *Interpretation* 41 (1987) 117–30.

Gustafson, James M. "The Place of Scripture in Christian Ethics: A Methodological Study," *Interpretation* 24 (1970) 430–55.

Hamerton-Kelly, Robert G. "Attitudes to the Law in Matthew's Gospel: A Discussion of Matthew 5:18," *Biblical Research* 17 (1972) 19–32.

Hanssen, Olav. "Zum Verständnis des Bergpredigt," *Der Ruf Jesu und die Antwort der Gemeinde*. E. Lohse, ed. Göttingen: Vandenhoeck & Ruprecht, 1970, 94–111.

Horsley, Richard A. "Ethics and Exegesis: 'Love Your Enemies' and the Doctrine of Non-Violence," *JAAR* 54 (1986) 3–31.

Keck, Leander. "Ethics in the Gospel According to Matthew," *Iliff Review* 40 (1984) 39–56.

Kingsbury, Jack D. "The Place, Structure and Meaning of the Sermon on the Mount Within Matthew," *Interpretation* 41 (1987) 131–43.

———. "The Verb AKOLOUTHEIN ("To Follow") as an Index of Matthew's View of His Community," *JBL* 97 (1978) 56–73.

Lischer, Richard. "The Sermon on the Mount as Radical Pastoral Care," *Interpretation* 41 (1987) 157–69.

Stanton, Graham. "The Gospel of Matthew and Judaism," *BJRL* 66 (1984) 264–84.

Tannehill, Robert. "The 'Focal Instance' as a Form of New Testament Speech: A Study of Matthew 5:39b–42," *Journal of Religion* 50 (1970) 372–85.

White, Leland. "Grid and Group in Matthew's Community: The Righteousness/Honor Code in the Sermon on the Mount," *Semeia* 35 (1986) 61–90.

Wink, Walter. "Beyond Just War and Pacifism: Jesus' Nonviolent Way," *Review and Expositor* 89 (1992) 197–214.

Yoder, John. "The Political Axioms of the Sermon on the Mount," *The Original Revolution*. Scottdale: Herald, 1971, 34–51.

Other Books in This Series